SEEDS FOR THE SOUL

*This book is dedicated to my brother Paul and his wife Maria
and their three children Daniella, Dominic and Sean.
They are my closest family and their love enables me
to continually look at life with eyes of faith.
They repeatedly show me how the seeds of faith can be nourished
and brought to fruit.
Thank you.*

Brendan McGuire

Seeds for the Soul

SUNDAY HOMILIES FOR CYCLE B

the columba press

First published in 2005 by
the columba press
55A Spruce Avenue, Stillorgan Industrial Park,
Blackrock, Co Dublin

Cover by Bill Bolger
Cover picture by Jed deTorres
Origination by The Columba Press
Printed in Ireland by ColourBooks Ltd, Dublin

ISBN 1 85607 509 5

Acknowledgements:
I am very grateful to the authors, editors and publishers of the follow-ing resources which have been inspirational to me and on which I have drawn in the course of preparing this book. I strongly recommend them to readers: *Celebration: An Ecumenical Worship Resource,* (Kansas City, Montana: National Catholic Reporter Company, Inc.); *Connections* (Mediaworks, Londonderry, NH.); *Homily Helps,* (St Anthony Messenger Press: Cincinnati, OH.); Brian Cavanaugh, *The Sower's Seeds,* and *Fresh Packet of Sower's Seeds,* (Mahwah, New Jersey: Paulist Press, 1990); DeMello, Anthony SJ, *One Minute Nonsense,* (Chicago: Loyola University Press, 1992); Fr Damien Dougherty OFM, *Scripture Commentaries for Christmas,* (Online through liturgy.com); James S. Hewett, *Illustrations Unlimited,* (Wheaton, New York: Tyndale House Publishers, 1988); Jude Siciliano OP, *Preachers Exchange,* (Raleigh, NC: preachex@opsouth.org); Liam Lawton, *Light the Fire,* (Chicago, IL: GIA Publications, 1995); Nicky Gumbel, *Questions of Life,* (Cook Communications Ministries: Colorado Springs, Colorado, 1996); Walter J. Burghardt SJ, *Tell the Next Generation,* (New Jersey: Paulist Press,1980); William F. Maestri, *Grace Upon Grace,* (Makati, Philippines: St Paul Publications, 1988); William J. Bausch, *Story Telling the Word,* and *More Telling Stories Compelling Stories,* (Mystic, Connecticut: Twenty-Third Publications, 1996).

Contents

Introduction

I believe that God's ways are mysterious yet understandable, hidden yet knowable, and divine yet human. In the struggle to understand God's ways we need to reflect on his role in our lives. The only way we experience life is through our human and fragile efforts, and so, it is in the midst of the ordinariness of life that I believe God speaks to us. He speaks loudly yet clearly if 'we have ears to hear.' Throughout the gospels, Jesus speaks in parables that are enigmatic, yet comprehensible; his meaning is concealed, yet intelligible; the knowledge he shares emanates from God, yet is for us, with our human fallibility and frailty. Our task is to listen to God's Word, and then reflect on how his Word relates to our ordinary everyday lives.

The title of this book was inspired by the Parable of the Sower of Seeds, from Matthew 13. The seed of the Word of God is proclaimed every week at Mass throughout the world, but we still do not fully understand the power of God's Word in our lives. This book of homilies is my humble attempt to relate God's Word to the everyday life of people hearing the gospel. Nearly all of these homilies were given by me, in person, to communities of faith in San Jose and Santa Clara, California.

My hope is that the stories in this book will help those of you who read them find a place in your soul to plant the seed of God, and that somewhere, at some time, on your journey through life, you will allow God to water this seed and bring it to fruition. May God bless your reflection and the 'planting of the seed.'

Acknowledgements

Each week my homily for the Sunday Mass starts with a story that somehow breaks open the scripture readings. In order to allow my story and reflection thereon to have the most power, I write down what I want to say. In doing so I get a sense of what I do not want to say. Then, after it is edited several times, I send the homily via electronic mail to a list of people who have requested it. One of those friends, Audry Lynch, an author herself, asked me to consider collecting my weekly homilies and getting them published. She then put me in contact with Seán O Boyle of The Columba Press. To Audry, I thank you for your encouragement and confidence in these homilies. Thank you to Seán O Boyle and Brian Lynch for their patience with me.

As part of the process of developing the right message, each week I 'bounce' my ideas off some friends. Many thanks to Sr Kathleen Hanley who gave me important feedback on several homilies. And for the last few years, Jed DeTorres has listened patiently, critiqued gently and reacted strongly to my ideas. I wish to express my gratitude to him for his patience, kindness and inspiration; his wisdom is now embedded in these homilies. The cover of this book was also designed by Jed DeTorres.

I thank the Jesuits at El Retiro Retreat House in Los Altos, California, especially Fr Bill Rewak, who gave me refuge from the busyness of my parish to get this book started. Also, I thank Pat and Ortwin Krueger for their incredible gift of hospitality at the Vineyard Country Inn, St Helena, California, as Friday after Friday I finished this book in peaceful surroundings.

Additionally, I want to thank the staff and parishioners of Holy Spirit Parish in San Jose, California for their support over the last year and a half. They have given me inspiration by their display of faith, especially those in the daily Mass community. In a special way I want to acknowledge Kelly Raftery-Piunti, who spent endless hours editing and proofing the texts of these homilies. Without her help this book would not have been a reality.

Actively Waiting for the Lord

Once I was on retreat with the other priests of the Diocese of San Jose and our retreat master, former Archbishop of San Francisco John Quinn, gave us some priestly advice about how to stay healthy. Among other things he told us to always take an annual vacation. He added that we should not only take a vacation but also plan and prepare for it too. He maintained that preparing for and anticipating a vacation is at least half the joy.

To convince us, he told a story about a priest of the archdiocese who refused to take a vacation because he thought he did not need a break. So the bishop reminded him that even if he didn't need the break from the people, the people needed a break from him! So the priest took a vacation. But he never planned or prepared for it. Year after year it would be the same! On a certain day, the priest would decide to go on vacation without telling anybody. He would go to the airport and decide where he would go by seeing which flights were available that day. He gave no warning, there was no note, there was no message! Just gone – he was just gone!

Archbishop Quinn maintains that the priest misses the point of vacation. Planning and preparing is half the joy. He called this preparation 'active waiting'.

Every year the church celebrates the incarnation of Christ on 25 December and none of us need to be reminded about that date. However, the church also supplies a period of preparation because it realises that anticipation is half the joy! Advent is that time, a time to prepare and anticipate the coming of Christ. It is the time when we can get excited about Christmas.

When I say 'prepare for and anticipate Christmas', I do not mean that we buy more gifts and go shopping. While these things are not bad in themselves, we can get caught up in the consumeristic preparation for Christmas. Instead I am suggesting that we prepare spiritually for Christmas. As we hear in today's gospel, Be Alert! Be Watchful! Today and this week we are being called to prepare and actively wait for the coming of Christ.

We prepare as individuals and as a community. The Advent

wreath which we will light in a moment is a sign of our waiting
and anticipation of Christmas. In the same way that we anticipate the coming of a vacation, we anticipate the coming of Christ
again in glory, and as each week passes we light another candle
and get a little more excited. Christ is coming! Of course, we
recognise and celebrate that Christ has already come in history
as a man. In the same way that we continue doing our work
while we prepare for our future vacation, we celebrate Christ's
presence among us here and now while we anticipate his return
in glory. So how do we prepare individually or as a community?

One of the ways we have suggested that we prepare this
Advent is through the giving of a gift to a child whose family
cannot afford it. And so we have the 'giving tree' in the vestibule
and ask that each of us find some way to give to a child in need.[1]
We also will be distributing prayer books for Advent, hoping
that we will all spend a little more time in prayer. Maybe we can
have our own Advent wreath at home and say a prayer before
each meal. Or maybe we can find someone in our family or
neighbourhood who needs something this Christmas or needs
someone to visit them.

We are challenged again today to prepare ourselves for
Christ, to prepare a place for Christ in our own heart. This is
where half the joy of the Christian life is. We can do this by
prayer, giving, or sharing of our time and so actively wait for the
Lord.

---

1. The 'giving tree' is a tradition in churches in the USA whereby fami-
lies-in-need put their wish list of gifts for their children on little cards
which are then placed on this tree. The parish purchases the gifts,
wraps them and delivers them to the families.

Extra! Extra! Read All About It!

When I was growing up in Ireland, there was a man who sold newspapers outside the front of the church. No matter what the weather, even pouring rain, the old man would be there, selling the papers. He was nicknamed 'Chicken,' because he always called out, 'Extra! Extra! Read all about it! Extra! Extra! Read all about it!' And when he did, he sounded like a squawking chicken. Chicken sold morning papers and evening papers and almost everyone in town would buy their daily papers from him, eager to read the latest breaking news. I know people who did not usually buy the newspaper, but when they heard Chicken they would always get one.[1]

As we hear the scripture for today, the second Sunday of Advent, we can almost hear the people of the day shouting, 'Extra! Extra! Read all about it!' If there were newspapers in Jesus' time, then surely he would have made the headline news! The event of God becoming human in Jesus Christ is not just an editorial comment but is, in fact, the headline news. The headline in the local paper would have read something like: 'The Word has become flesh. He now lives among us!' The reason so many people came to the desert to hear John the Baptist was to hear him declare the latest breaking news. God becoming human in Jesus Christ was the event of the decade, the century, and the millennium; it was the event that would change the world forever. Now that is not just regular news – It is good news! And it's not just good news – It is great news!

John the Baptist knew the news and he proclaimed it wildly: 'Extra! Extra! Hear all about it! The Messiah is here and lives among us now! Repent and turn away from sin!' John the Baptist made ready the way for the Lord by spreading the good news and sharing the joy of the truth. And we are called to do likewise in our lives. If this news is true, that Jesus Christ is the Son of God, that God became human and dwelt among us,

---

1. Adapted from Patricia Datchuck Sanchez, *Celebration: An Ecumenical Worship Resource*, (Kansas City, Montana: National Catholic Reporter Company, Inc., December, 2002).

that he lived and then died for our sins, that he rose from the dead and showed us eternal life, then it is not just news, but rather it is great news. So we need to communicate not only the power of the message but, like John the Baptist, we need to communicate the joy of the truth. We need to proclaim it wildly.

I believe to be authentic proclaimers of the good news we need to be purveyors of good attitude. I mean that in some way we need to be happy people – people full of joy, people who spread joy in the lives of others. Often I think we are lifeless about our faith. We mope around with sorrowful looking faces saying, 'Yeah, I'm Catholic.' Or 'Yes, I believe in God and am a Christian.' It is not convincing to our friends, or anyone for that matter, because we don't look convinced! If it is true, and we believe it is, that Jesus Christ the Son of God came among us and showed us the way, then we are no longer to be afraid of sin or death or life. Christ lives among us, within us now, and we have been saved. That is great news! In that case we need to be on fire with the Holy Spirit and allow the joy of Christ to pervade us. Then, when people look at us they will say we are one of two things – either we are crazy or we are Christians. But we cannot be in between; we need to be one or the other! We are either crazy or we are Christian to believe in Christ Jesus.

As we prepare for this Christmas season of peace and joy, we ought to find some way to spread the joy of the gospel. We need to be on fire with the Holy Spirit! We need to be contagious with joy! That sort of joy only comes from the Lord. Even if it is just to our family and friends, this season let us be purveyors of the good news. Let our lives proclaim the joy of Christ. And when others see us they should say that we are not crazy, but we are Christians. Extra! Extra! Read all about it! Jesus Christ is here!

Heeeeeeere's Jesus!

For three decades, every weekday night America heard announcer Ed McMahon introduce Johnny Carson. But Ed McMahon didn't do an ordinary introduction! The introduction was a cheerful call of joy in his voice: 'Heeeeere's Johnny!' Yes. That two-word announcement became part of the American scene and a hallmark of the 'Tonight Show.' Ed McMahon did not host the show. He always introduced Johnny as the host of the show.[1]

In today's gospel, John the Baptist introduces Jesus. John prepares the way for the Lord. John the Baptist is not the Messiah, but he points to the Messiah. He is not the light, but came to testify to the light. Never once does he claim to be the 'Anointed One!' Instead, he announces the new way to be found through Jesus. He does it with great joy in his heart. Maybe if he were here today he would say, 'Heeeeeeere's Jesus!'

When Paul writes to the Thessalonians he tells them to have constant joy. He encourages them to pray unceasingly, with never-ending thanks to God. He guides them not to quench the Spirit of Christ within them, but to recognise the good and turn away from evil. Paul encourages them to joyfully prepare for the Lord's coming.

Today we celebrate the third Sunday of Advent and we light the rose-coloured candle in our Advent wreath, the candle symbolising 'joy.' We are called not only to prepare for the Lord in our lives, but also to prepare for his coming joyfully.

Around this time each year we prepare for Christmas in many different ways. We write cards, we buy presents, we visit relatives, we attend parties and dinners, and we decorate our homes and offices. All of this can be great preparation for the coming of our Lord. However, we need to seek a balance with the true preparation – the preparation for the coming of Christ in glory and the recognition of Christ's presence in our hearts. If we can find a balance between how we prepare as a community

---

1. Dick Folger, *Celebration: An Ecumenical Worship Resource*, (Kansas City, Montana: National Catholic Reporter Company, Inc., December, 2002).

here, in our church, and how we prepare as a community out there, in our homes and offices, then I think we will have lived the Spirit of Christmas more fully.

Sometimes, we may end up preparing for the coming of Christ with reluctant hearts. We may grudgingly write our Christmas cards, grumbling about how long the list gets every year and how the people we write to never return the favour of a card. We may unenthusiastically attend dinners or visit friends or family, complaining about the company. We may resentfully buy gifts for family or friends, suspicious about what we will get in exchange.

Rather than this bleak preparation for Christmas, we should instead live the joyful spirit of the gospel by transforming how we prepare for Christmas. We can prepare with joyful hearts! First, we need to recognise the 'good' in our lives, as Paul says. If we have numerous gifts to get for family members, then we can be thankful that we have a family to care for. We can be thankful that our parents are still alive and we can buy for them. We can be thankful that we have children to whom we can show affection. If we have lots of cards to write or we have too many parties to go to, then we can be grateful that we have so many friends.

This Christmas season we can joyfully ready ourselves for the Lord by transforming the way we already prepare. We can willingly write to our family and friends. We can enthusiastically attend gatherings and visit with friends. We can gratefully buy gifts for family. These last weeks before Christmas may we truly prepare the way for the Lord, and announce with joy by our actions, attitudes and words: 'Heeeeeeere's Jesus!'

Yes, I will Lord

I remember Christmastime three years ago, when I was in my last year of training for priesthood. Many priest friends had said to me that the last year is the easiest. That was not my experience! Actually, I found it to be the toughest! This wasn't because the classes were difficult but because the last year is the final opportunity to drop out and leave formation and say, 'No, this is not for me. I cannot or will not become a priest.' In January of the last year, candidates for priesthood are ordained as deacons, and it is in this ceremony that we promise celibacy, obedience, and a life of simple living. It is then that we promise publicly to do God's will as a member of the church's leadership.

It became difficult for me as I reflected on those promises and I found myself doubting whether I could really do it. That I could really live without a family of my own, live without total control over my own life, live without a high paying job as a businessman. I doubted whether I wanted to do it at all!

In conversation with my spiritual director that week something came to light that struck to the heart of my dilemma. He said, 'Brendan, if you really believe God wants you to be a businessman then you must go. Do whatever God wants you to do. Priest or businessman, God gives us the help to do his will.' Without hesitation I snapped, 'This has nothing to do with God's will. I know what God wants. He wants me to be a priest. This has to do with what 'I' want. I want …'

I stopped mid-sentence. Suddenly I realised what was going on. As much as I was trying to do God's will, I was still trying to do it my way. I was still saying 'I want Lord,' instead of saying 'I will Lord.'

I think we all struggle at some time with doing God's will in our lives. Sometimes we say 'I want Lord' instead of saying 'I will Lord.' But this 'I will Lord' is not a once off decision. It is a daily commitment to saying yes to the Lord. Each day we have to choose to say yes. Each day I have to choose to say yes to my priesthood. In the same way, a couple who said yes on their wedding day each day chooses to say yes to each other. Or a single person choosing to remain chaste each day has to say, 'I will.'

And some days that is not easy for any of us.

Over these last three weeks we have celebrated Advent as a time of waiting and preparing for Christ's birth and his return in glory. Today we light the fourth Advent candle that symbolises the transition into Christmas itself. Today we hear in the gospel of the perfect example to how to say, 'yes, I will.' Mary exemplifies what every Christian is called to do. 'She is the perfect Christian.'[1] In her response to the angel's request saying, 'Let it be done unto me as you say,' she conceived Jesus within her womb. She said 'Yes, my Lord' – And lived that the rest of her life. I believe we too can conceive the Christ within us, by simply responding 'Yes, my Lord' each day.

While Mary's 'yes' brought about the incarnation in a specific time and place, our 'yes' can make God incarnate here and now in our own lives. It is the joyful yes that will transform the commercial reproduction Christmas we see in the world into the real Christmas celebration where God's will is lived out. So this week, in the midst of all the busyness of our lives, maybe we can bring Christ alive today by saying a joyful 'Yes, my Lord. I will.'

---

1. Walter J. Burghardt, SJ, *Tell the Next Generation*, (New Jersey: Paulist Press,1980) 199.

Icon of Christ

The 'icon' is an ancient religious art form that the church holds as a treasure. An Icon (from the Greek *eikon*, 'image') is an artistic visual representation or symbol of anything considered holy and divine. Many of our old churches are populated with these visual delights, which add sacredness to their spaces.The most treasured religious icons are those depicting images of Mary as Mother of God and Christ the Pantocrator. The image of Christ Pantocrator ('Christ, Ruler of All') was one of the first images of Christ developed in the Early Christian Church, and remains a central icon of the Eastern Orthodox Church. Christ holds the New Testament in his left hand and blesses the viewer with his right.[1]

Icons draw the person looking at them into the art itself. There is something magnificent about their beauty that defies words. When one spends a few moments gazing into an icon, one is drawn beyond its immediate image and into the reality it signifies. One is drawn to God. One is drawn into God and the reality of the divine. Of course, that can be said of any good religious art or any great art for that matter. However, there seems to be something particularly sacred about icons; they are almost windows to the sacred.

Tonight we celebrate the birth of Christ and the reality of God becoming human in Christ. We acknowledge that Christ is an icon of God. Christ gives us a unique window to our sacred God. When we look at Christ, we are drawn to him. When we look at Christ, we are drawn beyond the image and we see the God who sent him. When we look at Christ, we are called to see and know God in God's own self.

Luke's description of Jesus' actual birth scene is like an icon painting. Jesus is in a manger with straw, and Mary and Joseph are homeless in a foreign town. This barren scene highlights the stark poverty, genuine humility, and extreme simplicity surrounding Christ's birth. The shepherds are the first to receive the good news of the birth of the Messiah. At the time of Christ, shepherds were despised and commonly held incapable of

1. Definition from http://en.wikipedia.org/wiki/Icon

being witnesses, due to their unsavory reputation among the general public.[2] And, yet, to such as these and through them, God wants the first joyful news to arrive. Jesus, who is God, has now made his message known to all people. Jesus, who is God, is now human in all his vulnerabilities. Jesus, who is God, points to the God who made all humans. Jesus, who is God, is the icon of God.

The angels' hymn of praise gives voice to our collective awe and reveals this God of glory and peace, this God of humanity, and this God of heaven and earth. This historic event of the incarnation is God's greatest moment in human history.

As the first reading from Isaiah says, we come as 'a people who walked in darkness; we have seen a great light.' We come in abundant joy and great rejoicing as if 'we have received a great harvest.' Tonight of all nights we come to acknowledge that fact of faith. Tonight of all nights we come to live that fact of faith. Tonight of all nights we come to become that fact of faith.

Yes, tonight we are called to not only look into the image of Christ the child and believe in God-made-human, but also to look beyond that icon and see God himself. Then we are called to become that image of Christ to others. We are called to become a living icon of Christ, by how we act towards others. This Christmas, as we celebrate the gift of our faith in God becoming one of us, we are called to be the living icon of Christ.

2. Fr Damien Dougherty, OFM, *Scripture Commentaries for Christmas*, (Online through liturgy.com)

Not Commuters But Companions

Recently I was on a trip travelling to San Antonio, Texas for a conference. While I was on board the plane I looked around the airplane and saw all these people who were travelling to the same city as I was. I realised I did not know them nor did they know me. Yet here we were in very close proximity for hours. Yes, I had casual greetings with some and a small conversation with others. But in reality we were 'completely disinterested in each other's welfare.'[1] Here we were, travelling physically close to each other, and yet we remained worlds apart in reality. We were not companions on a journey but mere commuters crowded together for a temporarily mutual goal – to reach our city of destination.

Today we celebrate the anniversary of our new beginning in salvation history, when God became human in Christ. Today we celebrate the birth of Christ and the beginning of a new way of travelling through life. Today we recognise that we are no longer commuters going through life, disinterested in each other's welfare. Instead we are co-pilgrims and companions on the journey of life. We are different people from different countries, with different languages and different customs, travelling at different speeds, but we are all travelling to the same God. We are not just commuters travelling together with a common goal of returning to God, but we are companions on that journey who care for each other as we travel. In God becoming one of us we have a new purpose to our journey of life. We know now that our journey will not end in death but in eternal life. We know now that our journey is a pilgrimage to see God. We know now that we are companions on that journey together.

So if today we are visiting this church for the first time, then it is a day to celebrate our beginning of the journey of life. If today we are here after a long time away from the church, then it is a day to celebrate our return to the pilgrimage of life.

---

1. Patricia Datchuck Sanchez, *Celebration: An Ecumenical Worship Resource*, (Kansas City, Missouri: National Catholic Reporter Company, Inc., May, 2005).

If today we are here even though we have doubts about our faith, then it is the day to renew our faith in God and his love for us. If today we are here even though we have significant dark places in our lives, then it is the day to allow Christ to shine his light of grace into our hearts. If today we are here after a year full of Eucharistic celebrations, then it is the day to celebrate that so many have joined us as companions. Today is the day to celebrate the gift of our common purpose, to be companions on this journey of life. Today is the day to remember that Christ became one with us, as the companion for our collective journey. So then, what must we do to be good companions on this journey?

While it wouldn't harm commuters in airplanes to be more courteous to one another, if we are to be companions on the journey of life it has to be about more than just courtesy and manners, though these things are important. We need to care about each other in a much deeper way as we travel through this life together. True companions concern themselves with other people for the sake of the welfare of the other person, ensuring that others have what they need for life. The root meaning of 'companion' is to 'break bread with.' It has to do with being 'one with' the other person. Today is the day to think of, pray for and be generous to others who share this same journey of life.

May we celebrate Christmas in a unique way this year by being not just commuters with each other but true companions on our journey of life.

Making Our Families Holy

Recently I had the opportunity to watch a movie called 'Family Man.' It is a delightful movie about a man who became a very successful businessman on Wall Street. Then one day he was given the opportunity to see how his life could have been, had he married his college girlfriend. His current life was marked with apparent success; he had authority over a large number of people, an extravagant condominium in New York City with a fancy car, and was a powerhouse on Wall Street. The other life as a family man was apparently less successful, with a small house in suburbia and a minivan for the kids.

Yet the first life was also marked with other characteristics, such as selfishness and self-absorption. It was a life of profound loneliness as well, and was a life lacking in meaning. Life as a family man was marked with other characteristics too, such as selflessness and serving others. It was a life full of meaning and jam-packed with joy. In the end, the man made his choice of which life he would rather lead. I believe the same can be said for all of us. We choose our priorities.

Today we celebrate the Feast of the Holy Family and we acknowledge a life full of meaning led by Joseph and Mary. We hear in the gospel how Joseph made his choice to be a family man and do as the Lord asked. In making this choice, Joseph and Mary led a life listening closely to God and making many sacrifices for their son. We also hear in the first and second readings how God promised Abraham reward if only he remained faithful to his call for him. While Abraham was an old man God promised him 'descendents as numerous as the stars in the sky and as countless as the sands on the seashore.' In faith, Abraham obeyed God and led God's people. In return, God gave him Isaac who was his cherished child, and through him, descendents too numerous to count. He sacrificed his life for God but was rewarded in manifold ways. We, too, will be rewarded when we live a life of service for the Lord. Sometimes that reward is here and now, other times it will be in the afterlife. Either way we are rewarded, God promises.

Many of you are fathers and mothers and you have made

many sacrifices for your children. Yet you know the rewards of being parents can be awesome. Good parents lead selfless lives, serving others in many ways. They tend to their children when they are sick. They cook meals for them every day. And when they are young, they clean their rooms and launder their clothes. They laugh at their jokes (which are sometimes not even funny) and cry when they are sad. Good parents serve their children. So as we acknowledge the presence and sacrifices of our parents, we acknowledge they chose to be family men and women. We can help them realise their reward here and now. We ought to recognise the gift of our own families. We ought to be thankful to our parents for choosing to be family-oriented people. We ought to be grateful for all the sacrifices our families have made for us. But today we are called to be grateful explicitly and to show them they are appreciated.

Maybe we have spent this Christmas with our parents, so we can give them an extra hug and tell them how much their love has meant to us. Maybe we did not see our parents this Christmas season, but we can call them in the next few days and express our gratitude for their many sacrifices. Or maybe we have not spoken with our parents in a long time. Then today of all days, we can call them and be reconciled with them. And if our parents have passed away, then we can pray for them this day.

Whatever way we choose, may we recognise the gift of our parents and how, by their sacrifices, they made our families holy.

God Makes Music with Us

Suzanne Farrell was a well-known ballerina who retired from the stage in 1988. While working with her, choreographer George Balanchine compared their relationship to that of a great violinist and a Stradivarius violin. For those of you not familiar with violins, Stradivarious violins are generally regarded to be the best in the world. Just as a great violinist when playing his/her virtuoso brings out the beautiful music from the Stradivarious, so Balanchine was able to call forth Ms Farrell's talents in her artistic dance. Ms Farrell brought an unusual humility to her profession. She preferred coming to the rehearsal of a new dance with little prior knowledge of the music. 'If I know the music too well beforehand,' she explained, 'I might tend to move in a certain way, and the choreographer would then have tear down that barrier.' Her humility freed the choreographer to bring out the best in her.[1]

Today, as we celebrate the Solemnity of Mary, Mother of God, we reflect again on the significance of God becoming a human being and the choice of Mary as the new beginning for humanity. Today, as we begin a New Year, we seek to be inspired anew. Mary, the mother of God, can also be compared to a Stradivarius in the hands of great violinist. Her humble response to God in saying 'yes, Lord' allowed God to send his Son into the world to save us. By Mary's humble assent to becoming the mother of the Son of God, God was able to play a symphony through humanity's history. By Mary's humble assent to becoming the mother of the Son of God, God gives us a new way back to him. Because of Mary's humble submission to God's will we begin this New Year with a new sense of hope for humanity. We have a new confidence in God that his will can be done among us throughout the year ahead. In Mary, God gives us a model of the way to be a humble disciple.

The gospel reading today says, 'Mary kept all these things, reflecting on them in her heart.' Mary somehow exuded a sense of peace and hope by her willing submission to allow God to do

---

1. *Homily Helps*, (St Anthony Messenger Press: Cincinnati, OH, May, 2005)

what he had to do. So then, how do we follow her humble way of being? How do we allow God to continue to play that symphony through our humble submission in our lives? Where do we start for our humble 'yes' to the Lord?

In today's first reading, Aaron and his sons, the priests of Israel, are told that they are to extend the blessing of God to the people. On this New Year's Day, the best place for us to start is to extend our peace to others and pray for peace throughout the world. We say to others 'may the Lord let his face shine upon you.' Or as we say in Ireland, may God 'smile upon you and your family.' The climax of this blessing is then peace: 'The Lord look upon you kindly and give your peace!' The Hebrew word for 'peace' is 'shalom,' which is a much more positive concept than the way that we usually think of peace. Peace in the Hebrew context means more than merely a lack of war. 'Shalom' is more to do with a well-being and harmony in one's relation to God, to one's self, and to one another. May God grant us the blessing of this peace in the New Year and may we become active members in that peace here on earth.

We allow God to continue to make wonderful music when we allow his peace to dwell within us and when we allow his peace to dwell within our relationships with others. This may mean that we ask forgiveness from someone we have hurt in the years past. Or this might mean that we grant forgiveness to someone who has hurt us in years past. Or maybe it is both! Today, as we begin this New Year, we seek a new sense of hope. Today we humbly submit to God's will in our lives. Today we bless others with God's peace. Today we allow God to make music with our lives.

Grace and Truth of Life

A woman was losing at the roulette wheel in a Las Vegas casino. When she was down to her last ten dollars, she asked the fellow next to her for a good number. 'Why don't you bet your age?' he suggested. The woman smiled shyly, and placed her last ten dollars on the table. When the roulette wheel came to a stop, the woman suddenly fainted and fell to the floor. The acquaintance who had given her the advice rushed over. 'Did she win?' he asked, as he helped her up. 'No,' replied the croupier, 'She put ten dollars on 29 but 41 came up.'[1]

The truth can be so difficult to face and accept. We often obfuscate, rationalise, or even deny the truth, rather than face some powerful fact that confronts us. It might be a truth about ourselves, our lives, our values, or our dreams. No matter what it is, sometimes the truth is very hard to face. Christ challenges us not to approach truth in terms of wins and losses, or power or convention, but rather in terms of how we can make his presence felt in the world, by the way we love one another.

The truth of this season of Christmas is that God became human in Christ. That is the central truth of faith – the incarnation. If we can face that reality and accept it in our hearts then it ought to change us completely. Think about it for just one moment: Our omnipotent God, who created the entire universe including us, became one of us and lived like us to show us the way through life on earth and to show us the way through death to eternal life. Christ who dwelt among us came to show us the way. Christ is the way, the truth and the life. The way through life. The way to life. The way through death. The way to eternal life. All of us who come to him will have life and truth to the fullest.

In today's gospel we hear how John the Baptist came to testify to the truth. John knew his role was to point the way to Christ and he did so at great cost to himself: his life. Yes, we believe that the fullness of life comes from and through Christ. 'From his fullness we have all received, grace in place of grace, because while the law was given through Moses, grace and truth came

---

1. *Connections* (Mediaworks, Londonderry, NH: April, 2005)

through Jesus Christ.' (Jn 1:17) So then, how do we live this grace and truth in our lives?

I think the first place we need to go is prayer. The truth can be so difficult to face and accept, but if we pray we can offset some of our rationalisation and denial. There, we can face the stark truth that may confront us. It might be a truth about ourselves, our lives, or our values, but whatever it is that we need to face, the truth and grace of Christ helps us on our way. Then we can move to a life of gratitude.

Maybe we take some advice from the Letter to the Ephesians. To live this truth of faith is to be thankful for our blessings and people in life. 'I do not cease giving thanks for you and remembering you in my prayers, that the God of our Lord Jesus Christ, and the Father of glory, may give you a Spirit of wisdom and revelation, resulting in knowledge of him.' So this week may we face the truth in our lives and give thanks to God in prayer for the gift of others.

Take the Risk and See the Light of Christ

Last year a friend of mine and I went to Yellowstone National Park. It is a beautiful place with many interesting sites. One such beautiful site is Shoshone Lake. Unfortunately, it was our last day and we had not seen it yet. The weather was poor; it rained heavily all morning until late afternoon, and a chance to see the lake was not looking good. Then around 5 pm the sun broke through the clouds a little, and I said to my friend that we should take the risk to hike the 5 miles to the lake before dark. He reminded me of the real danger of another thunderstorm and, more importantly, of the real danger of Grizzly bears who like to feed in the evening. After all, humans are good food!Well, we decided to take the risk anyway and we hiked with pep in our step through the evening twilight. When we arrived, the evening sun glistened on the water and the lake shone like a pot of gold at the end of a rainbow. It was truly magnificent! I will always remember that sight. On the way back, which we made in even quicker time, we congratulated each other on taking the risk despite impending dangers, recognising that we were truly rewarded for our efforts.

I think there are many times in our lives when we are presented with opportunities to do good and be part of something better. But we must be willing to take the risk and be willing to go for it. We must be willing to listen to the message and experience something new.

In today's gospel we hear about the Magi who saw the birth of a star. They believed that this heavenly wonder symbolised the birth of a heavenly person. They took a risk and followed that star as their sign. When they eventually got to their destination they were rewarded by seeing the newly born King of Jews, Jesus Christ. They discovered the new light of the world. And they were forever different! This conversion is symbolised by their change in the path they took on their return, avoiding King Herod to whom they once felt beholden. Now they were different. They had seen the light of Christ.

Today we celebrate the Solemnity of the Epiphany of the Lord, which signifies the manifestation of the light of Jesus

Christ, the revelation of Jesus Christ as the Saviour of the world. Isaiah reminds us of that symbolism when he says: 'Arise, shine, for the glory of the Lord has risen upon you.' (Is 60:1) This is a celebration of the bright light of Jesus Christ and a reminder that his light still shines today.

So, we are reminded of our baptism call to see his light shine in all. We are called to see signs of his presence among us. We are called to take the risk and follow his signs. We are called to discover Christ again. Each of us is different and we see different signs. Where is God guiding us this week? What risk do we need to take to see Christ's light?

Let me give you an example. Just before Christmas, our youth group here at this parish fed the homeless and hungry at a neighbouring parish. At first our group was nervous and a little afraid, but after returning the youth were different. Their faces shone brightly as they recalled their experience. They have seen the light of Christ in those they serve. Their lives are forever different. We, too, become different when we see the light of Christ present among us. We, too, are never the same. But we have to take the risk!

Maybe it is not feeding the homeless or hungry, but perhaps it is some other act of charity. Christmas holidays are always a time of family. When there is division in the family, this time of year can be difficult. This year, why don't we make the light of Christ shine in our families by forgiving someone or reconciling with someone.

Christ is calling us to move deeper into our relationship with him but we need to be willing to take the risk and follow him. This week, may our hearts be renewed in the Lord and may we take the risk to discover the light of Christ.

Call to be Consistent

This is my beloved Son, with whom I am well pleased. (Mt 3:17) Several centuries before Christ, Alexander the Great came out of Macedonia and Greece to conquer the Mediterranean world. He was a commander known for his military prowess. On one of his campaigns, Alexander received a message that one of his soldiers had been continually misbehaving and thereby casting a bad light on the character of all the Greek troops. And what made it worse was that this soldier's name was also Alexander. When Alexander the Great learned of this, he sent word that he wanted to talk to the errant soldier in person. When the young man arrived at his tent, Alexander the Great asked him, 'What is your name?' The reply came back, 'Alexander, sir.' The commander looked him straight in the eye and said forcefully, 'Soldier, either change your behaviour or change your name.'

When we call ourselves Christians, we are identifying with Jesus Christ. When we wear a cross, put Christian stickers on our cars, attend a Catholic school, or come to church on Sundays, we are being witnesses for him. We are answering the call to discipleship and being identified with the name Christ. But, is our behaviour compatible with being called Christian? Would Christ be happy with how we behave?[1]

Today the church celebrates the baptism of Jesus and we are also celebrating vocation awareness week. When John baptised Jesus it was more than a simple ritual, and it signified something deeper. It was the starting of a new mission in his life. This was a public event for all to see, something like getting married, or something like declaring one's candidacy, not for political public office, but for the public office of Christian, a follower of Jesus. So for Jesus himself, his baptism was not a cleansing from sin, but something deeper: a public declaration of his mission.[2]

---

1. James S. Hewett, *Illustrations Unlimited*, (Wheaton, New York: Tyndale House Publishers, 1988) 299-300.
2. Words paraphrased from William J. Bausch, *More Telling Stories Compelling Stories*, (Mystic, Connecticut: Twenty-Third Publications, 1997) 56

In a similar way, our baptism defines us publicly in relationship to God and to each another. It defines us as children of God
and enrolls us in the public office of 'Christians.' Indeed, each
time we enter the church we bless ourselves with holy water
from the baptismal font, as a symbol of baptismal renewal.
This is a reminder that we belong to Christ, not in a private way
but in a very public, and committed way. Therefore we always
need to be aware of our name: 'Christian.' Our actions ought always reflect who we are as Christians.

Back in Ireland there is a famous Protestant preacher called
Ian Paisley. He is famous not because of his lovely preaching
but because he encourages hatred in the words he speaks.
He blames the problems of Northern Ireland on the Catholics
and constantly exhorts violent resistance as their only solution.
It seems to me any person who claims to believe in gospels
ought to preach what Christ preached! Not only that, but also
ought to be willing to act accordingly – namely, to encourage
peace and love. It seems to me that we do Christ a great discredit
when our actions betray Christ's words and actions.

Of course nobody here is another Ian Paisley, but sometimes
we inadvertently participate in words of hatred. Often, we are
not aware of how our actions are different than our claims. For
example, when we gossip, we are speaking words of violence.
When we bad-mouth people, we are speaking words of violence.
When we categorise people into races and judge them by their
colour or by their accent, we are speaking words of violence.
There are many, many ways in which we can 'speak' words of
violence by our actions, and thus act not at all in the way Christ
showed us.

But by baptism, we are called to a personal relationship with
God, and a share in the responsibility of building the kingdom
of God. In other words, we ought to be willing to act Christian
as well as be called Christian. We are called to lead a Christian
life of holiness, yet we are all called in different ways. Some are
called to married life, others to single life, and still others are
called to lead Christian life in a more intense way, as ordained or
vowed religious in our church.[3]

So this week in response to the gospel, perhaps we can deter-

3. The Feast of the Baptism of the Lord always coincides with Vocation
Awareness Sunday in the USA and so there is an extra tie to our vocation in life.

mine what it is that God wants of us. Maybe we are called to an intense response, to live a religious or ordained life. If this call is great in you, talk with your parents or close friends, and then talk with a priest or religious. For all of us, we are called to lead a life of holiness. So, what actions can we take this week that would make this holiness evident to those around us? Is there a person at work whom we never greet, or maybe a family member we cannot forgive, or a neighbor who drives us crazy and is just too much!

Whatever the case may be, we are all baptised into Christ Jesus, and our Christian vocation is to lead a life of holiness. This week, let us ask what action we can change so that we can be more consistent in our lives as Christians, so our God can say of us, This is my beloved son or daughter in whom I am well pleased.

Prayer, Fasting, and Almsgiving

One Ash Wednesday a priest suggested that kids could clean up their rooms for Lent as penance. When one mother and her son got home, the mother reminded the child about the room. At first there was a little argument, but of course, the mother won the battle and soon the son went up to his room and started cleaning. Then suddenly, the boy came rushing to his mother saying, 'Mommy, I cannot do it!' 'Why?' asked the mother. 'Well,' the little boy continued, 'I'm too afraid! The priest said, 'We need to remember that we are dust and to dust we shall return.' I am afraid that there will be lots of people either going or coming from under my bed!'

Today we are celebrating the beginning of the Lent – Ash Wednesday, and Lent will end on Holy Thursday evening. This season begins with honest and solemn reflection about humanity, the humbleness of our beginning, and the simplicity of our departure. We are dust and to dust we shall return. Yes, our bodies came from nothing and they will return to nothing. But as Christians we believe that we are more than just flesh and bone. We believe in humble human beginnings, but we also believe in our divine destiny.

This time of Lent is a time to go deeper into our faith and realise the greatness of the destiny of humanity. It is a time to examine what we hold dear to our hearts, a time to plunge the depths of our own minds and souls, a time to strengthen our relationship with God. Lent is a time to reflect and examine our destiny as humans. It seems to me that the season of Lent stands on three legs: prayer, fasting, and almsgiving.

The first leg, that of prayer, has always been a foundation for us as believers. In this Lenten season we are challenged to take our prayer more seriously. Maybe that means praying a little more if we feel we do not pray enough. Or perhaps it means changing our prayer style; maybe we are challenged to say a prayer of thanks, as opposed to request. Or, we might be challenged to pray for forgiveness or healing. Yes, we are called to pray in Lent.

The second leg is fasting, which does not mean fast eating. It is not fast food like McDonald's or Burger King. Nor is it the bad dieting approaching of simply skipping our meals. Rather, like all other Lenten sacrifices, fasting ought to bring us into right relationship with God. The best fast is to give up whatever is blocking God's love in us. Maybe that is food or drink, but it very well might be an attitude! Perhaps it is an attitude of skepticism or cynicism from which we need to fast.

The last leg of Lent is almsgiving. Almsgiving is not simply giving something to the poor, but rather it is an attitude of sharing with other people. This could mean lending a listening ear to someone who needs it, or maybe accepting an apology from someone. Almsgiving is not only giving but it is also sharing.

These three legs of Lent will produce in us three fruits. Prayer encourages us to deepen our relationship with God. Fasting enhances our self-discipline and self-control. Almsgiving improves our relationship with each other.

And so as we line up today to receive the ashes on our foreheads, be mindful of the message of the three legs of lent: prayer, fasting, and almsgiving, all of which lead us to a better relationship with God, with ourselves and with others.

We are dust and to dust we shall return.

Time Out!

When I visit my brother and his family, my niece and nephew are always excited to see 'Uncle Father Brendan.' There is general bedlam when I arrive! Inevitably either Dominic or Daniella go too far with their fun and get their first warning, and then a second. Finally, they are warned for the last time with a time-out! Even though they know they are getting in trouble they continue their bedlam anyway, almost with a certain amount of enjoyment as they look at their dad and act wildly one more time. Then my brother will say 'time-out' and off they go to the corner. My brother will ask them to think about what they have done and then he talks with them before the end of the time-out. Does that sound familiar to you parents?

Child psychologists point out that children need 'time-outs', and not because they are in league with the Devil. A child's misbehaviour is often a result of frustration or excitement; they may not know how to deal with a situation, or they may not be able to control their emotions, or they may not understand how their behaviour affects others.

Learning experts suggest that parents should discipline not to punish but to teach. Instead of telling the child, 'You shouldn't have done that,' it is better to ask, 'Do you realise what you did?' This teaches children to take responsibility for their own actions. At an early age they learn that their actions have consequences.[1]

Well, the church supplies us with a time-out called Lent. This discipline is not punishment but rather a teaching moment for all of us. We are called to learn more about ourselves. We are called to ask ourselves, 'Do I realise what I have done recently?' Just as the Spirit drove Jesus to the desert, so the Spirit drives us to the desert of Lent.

I love the gospel of Mark about Jesus' trip to the desert. The Evangelist Mark adds nothing extra in telling his story. Mark's gospel is the shortest and he always gets straight to the point. The three-fold point in today's gospel is that:

(1) the Spirit drove Jesus into the desert;

---

1. Adapted from *Connections* (Mediaworks, Londonderry, NH: March, 2003)

(2) Jesus spent 40 days there being tempted;

(3) Jesus started his ministry immediately following his desert experience.

We, too, are called to 'time-out' and enter into some self-imposed time in the desert, so that we can listen to God and find out our call to ministry. The church gives us three ways to focus our energies for this Lenten journey of conversion called *metanoia* – a change of mind. The three ways are prayer, fasting and almsgiving.

The 'time-out' of Lent is our opportunity to focus on more intense prayer, using prayer to turn back towards God and reflect on our actions. Do our actions match our words and values? Do we realise what we have done?

Second, we are called to fasting. We fast from some food not because hunger is a good thing. No, we fast to identify with the people who are hungry. Years ago when I was growing up in Ireland, the religiously minded would say, 'think of those poor children in Africa who will have no food today.' Well, I want to tell you that we do not need to go that far! There are over 1 million children in the USA who will go without a meal today because they cannot afford it. There will be hundreds, if not thousands, of children in our local community who will go hungry today. Indeed, I will tell you that there are children in our very own Catholic schools who will come into school hungry and we need to feed them before we finish the day.

The problem of hunger is closer than we think. And it is not a good thing. Hunger is not a good thing! So when we fast, we identify with others so that we can change our hearts and change our minds about how we deal with those who go hungry every day. This is not to glamorise hunger but to come to an understanding of the reality of those in hunger.

That is where the third part of Lent comes in – almsgiving. After we identify with the poor or hungry, then we are moved to help them. We can give alms with our money, yes – and that is important – but how about also giving it with our time or talent?

This Lent, maybe we can push ourselves to take a 'time-out' and pray a little more intensely, fast a little more justly, and give a little more generously, in all ways.

Yogurt Slip!

When immigrants from Norway and Sweden came to the United States in the early 1900s, they brought with them 'yogurt,' a staple of their Scandinavian diet. But they brought the yogurt in the form of what they called 'yogurt slips.' A yogurt slip was a small, clean piece of white flannel that had been dipped in yogurt and dried in the sunshine. The cloth, just a few inches square, dried like a stiff piece of cardboard. Then it was stored for their travels. When they arrived in their new home here in America, the Norwegians and the Swedish would put their yogurt slip into a glass of warm milk. The yogurt culture contained in the cloth would be activated and would turn the milk into yogurt. You see, the culture of yogurt always remains alive.[1]

Within each one of us, we possess the Spirit of God's compassion and justice, a Spirit that enables us to 'transfigure' our world. Dwelling within us is the 'live culture' of God's grace. Too often I think we just remain mere 'slips,' unwilling or unable to bring the 'culture' of grace into the mix of the work and school and play.

On the mountain of transfiguration, the disciples saw in Jesus the very life and love of God that dwelled within him. They saw him for who he really is, the Messiah, and the fulfillment of the Law and the prophets represented by Moses and Elijah.

That same love of God lives within each of us as well, calling us beyond our own needs, wants, and interests. This love of God calls us beyond ourselves – first to transform us, and then, to transform our world. When Jesus Christ came here to our world he brought within himself the 'culture' of grace from God. He immersed himself completely into the world as a human so that the 'live culture' of God's grace could be activated fully into humanity.

It is that same 'culture' we take here at this table each Sunday. We take away with us each week a 'slip' of Jesus Christ and are called to then bring it into our lives around us and trans-

---

1. *Connections* (Mediaworks, Londonderry, NH: March, 2003)

form our world each week. These elements of bread and wine are not simply bread and wine, but are truly the 'live culture' of Jesus' body and blood.

So we are called not to just come here to church, hang out for a while, and then leave Jesus here. No, we are called to bring the living Jesus, that live culture of grace, into our work places, into our schools, into our families, and into our world wherever that takes us. We are called to transfigure or transform our world today.

We do this by first allowing that culture of grace to be activated, allowing his Spirit to become alive within. Then we, like Jesus, are called to immerse ourselves completely so that same Spirit can transform our lives, our family, and our community.

We transform our world by being there for those in need; by being a person of faith when someone's faith is shaken by life's trials; by being a person of joy when someone is overwhelmed by sadness of loss; by being a person of healing when someone needs forgiveness; by being a person of welcome when someone feels lonely or left out; and by being a person of love when someone feels unloved.

So this week let us be a 'yogurt slip' for the gospel and immerse ourselves in this celebration of this Eucharist, and then immerse ourselves in the world in which we live. We can transform our lives, our family, our community, and our world by being the 'culture' of grace.

Get Rid of the Old
to Make Room for the New

When I was going through my formation as a priest, I had to move every year. So for five years in a row I moved all my belongings from my house to the Graduate Theological Union, Berkeley, from Berkeley to the University of Notre Dame, from Notre Dame to the seminary, from the seminary to the parish house for a pastoral year, from the parish back to the seminary, and finally, from the seminary to this parish. To be honest I am very happy I have not moved for the last three years!

In all that moving I realised that I had a lot of 'stuff' and each year I would try to rid myself of some 'stuff'. So I came up with a rule: if I have not used it since I last moved, then I give it away. Every year I got rid of tons of 'stuff'. After arriving here I wanted to keep my stuff at a minimum, so I have a new rule: every time I buy something new, like a new pair of pants, then I must give away an old pair of pants. So to make room for the new stuff I get rid of some old stuff. While I do not always succeed, for the most part it works really well.

Well, I think the same could be said for our spiritual lives. We hold onto a lot of stuff that makes us less mobile. And we keep collecting stuff and become burdened by it. If we are honest, we know we have only so much room in our lives. We need to get rid of something to make room for Jesus Christ. That is what this Lenten season is about – conversion of our own hearts.

In today's gospel we hear how Jesus comes into the temple and gets rid of the old way to make room for the new way – himself! He is outraged that the temple, the place of worship, has turned into something of a marketplace. In anger, he turns over the tables of the money-changers and tells them to get out of the temple, the place of worship.

Not everyone is ready to hear this new way of Jesus Christ. The Pharisees and scribes were not! They questioned Jesus. But they misunderstood Jesus' comments. Jesus will be the new temple! Jesus himself, the risen Lord, will be the body where God's presence will dwell forever. We are called to worship him and take his presence within us, making us the temple of the Holy Spirit too.

We are called to convert our own lives to Jesus Christ. We are called to get rid of the old stuff in our hearts and make room for the temple of the Holy Spirit. As you know, during this Lenten journey we are invited to fast, to engage in more intense prayer, and to share with our brothers and sisters. But if we are to do these authentically then we need to make room for Christ.

For example, if we are to pray more, let's say ten minutes extra a day, then somehow we have to get rid of something we are currently doing. Few of us have extra time every day! Maybe we eliminate ten minutes of TV viewing or book reading, or perhaps we cut down on time spent reading newspapers or talking on the phone. We have to get rid of something to make room for Christ.

Where else can we make room for Christ in our lives? What tables do we need to turn over to make room for him? Maybe we need to turn over the table of unforgiveness and make room for reconciliation. Maybe we need to turn over our destructive friendships and start some new friendships in Christ. Maybe we need to turn over the pain of self-hatred and realise that we are made in God's own image. Maybe we need to turn over the old perceptions of God from childhood and realise that we are called to grow and mature in our faith.

Today we can make a new rule in our lives and decide that we will take something new from Christ. But first we need to make room for Christ. Today, may we get rid of some old 'stuff' to make room for the new 'stuff' called Christ.

Be Patient! God is Not Finished With Us Yet!

Many of the great works of art have never been finished. Take, for example, the unfinished sculptures of Michelangelo or many of the great European Cathedrals – they are unfinished, and this is part of their strange beauty. Most of these great artists left their work unfinished deliberately, making the statement that God alone can make them complete or perfect.[1]

In a sense, we too are incomplete. God created us and considered his creation good, indeed very good. But we are made not perfect. I do not think any of us need any examples of the ways in which we are not perfect. I believe we already know that, maybe too well!

But we are made good and there are plenty of examples of that too. Life here on earth is our opportunity to become perfect or complete. We are on our way to perfection or completion. I recently saw a bumper sticker on the back of a car, 'Be patient. God is not finished with me yet!' In a sense, we are all works of art in progress.

To use the words of scripture from today's second reading from Paul's letter to the Ephesians, we are God's handiwork. The Greek word for handiwork is *poema*, which means something that a person makes. Or, as another way of putting it, we are hand-made! We are hand-made by God with love.

Poema is the root word for poem. So we are God's work of art or piece of poetry. In the same way each poem is unique, so too are we. No two poems are the same. No two humans are the same. And just as a good poem reaches its completion in the reciting or reading of it, so too we reach our completion when we act as Christ intended us to.

We are God's work of art in progress. No, God is not finished with us; he is not finished with us individually and is not finished with us as a people. This work of art has been going on for centuries, as the first reading from Chronicles validated.

Time and time again, the people of Israel were warned by the

---

1. *Homily Helps*, (St Anthony Messenger Press: Cincinnati, OH, March, 2003)

prophets, and today we are reminded by scripture, that God came to save us. God continues to call humanity to conversion. Within each one of us this art-in-progress still continues today, if we allow God to work. The very key is that we allow the work to continue.

What we are is a gift from God to us. What we become is our gift back to God. We were made good, very good, and we must believe that first. We come to this table today to offer thanks to God for the gift that he made to each of us.

We also come to this table to offer ourselves as sacrifice and lay down our sins before him. We come to gain the strength to allow him to continue his work of art. The process of letting God continue his work is called *metanoia*, or conversion, of our own minds and hearts. It is the focus of the Lenten journey.

As we hit mid-point in our Lenten journey, we must ask ourselves where in our lives do we need to make progress. To be effective in our *metanoia*, we need to hear where God is calling forth growth. This calls for prayer and reflection about lives.

When we pray we are called to be honest and to ask, what are my weaknesses and how can I make progress? Yes, we acknowledge our strengths and weaknesses so that God can continue the good work he has started in us. This is really God's work, gift, and grace. We are all works of art in progress. May we be patient as God finishes his work of art.

Fifth Sunday of Lent
Jer 31:31-34; Ps 51; Heb 5:7-9; Jn 12:20-33

The Road Less Travelled

I was out hiking recently at one of my favorite places, Rancho San Antonio. As many of you may know, it is a busy spot because of its close proximity to 'Silicon Valley,' California. When I go there I always try to hike on trails that are less busy than others. This week I took one that was definitely less travelled! But I soon found out why it was less travelled – it was very, very difficult. It seemed to be uphill all the way, even on the way back! It reminded me of that poem by Robert Frost, *The Road Not Taken*.[1] It is a short but beautiful poem and I would like to share it with you today.

> Two roads diverged in a yellow wood,
> And sorry I could not travel both
> And be one traveller, long I stood
> And looked down one as far as I could
> To where it bent in the undergrowth;
> Then took the other, as just as fair,
> And having perhaps the better claim,
> Because it was grassy and wanted wear;
> Though as for that the passing there
> Had worn them really about the same,
> And both that morning equally lay
> In leaves no step had trodden black.
> Oh, I kept the first for another day!
> Yet knowing how way leads on to way
> I doubted if I should ever come back.
> I shall be telling this with a sigh
> Somewhere ages and ages hence:
> Two roads diverged in a wood, and I –
> I took the one less travelled by,
> And that has made all the difference.[2]

Jesus most certainly took the road less traveled – to always obey his Father's will. We know for ourselves that doing the Father's

---

1. Concept of Robert Frost's poem was germinated from Patricia Datchuck Sanchez, *Celebration: An Ecumenical Worship Resource*, (Kansas City, Montana: National Catholic Reporter Company, Inc., April, 2003).
2. Robert Frost, 'The Road Not Taken,' from William Harmon, Ed., *The Top 500 Poems* (New York: Columbia University Press, 1992).

will is not always easy. We know that it is the road less travelled!

In today's gospel we hear how Jesus said, 'Unless a grain of wheat falls to the ground and dies, it remains just a grain of wheat. But if it dies, it produces much fruit.' We are called to die, to let go of our own selfish needs and live for others instead. It means letting go of our old selves, old routines, and habits and being open to new ways and new risks of being Christian. This 'dying' is what we call 'conversion'; it is a continual changing of our lives; it is a continual letting go of the old ways; it is never resting with the *status quo*. When we choose to let go of our old ways and say yes to new ways, then we are choosing one path over another.

Yes, we are called to choose the road less travelled—the Christian road. In the same way, I set out hiking on that trail used less by others and realised that it was a more difficult trail. When we choose the Christian road, we realise it is not an easy one. This choice happens once at our baptism and initiation into the church. But if we are true followers of Jesus Christ, then it happens every single day. Yes, we chose it today and we are here because of it.

But tomorrow we will need to choose it again and then again on Tuesday, and on Wednesday, and so on until next Sunday when we return here to be strengthened again at this table.Yes, we must choose the Christian road each day in our actions. When we say yes to one thing, then we say no to another. When we choose to use words of kindness and patience and not words of judgement and prejudice, we choose the right path. When we choose to use words of forgiveness or tolerance instead of words of unforgiveness or hatred, we choose the right path. Whether with our neighbors or friends or children or parents, or even with people we do not know, we proclaim, by our actions, the choice of the road we travel. Yes, when we act in goodness we are on the road less travelled, the Christian road, and it will make all the difference.

Stay Connected!

I hold in one hand a battery and in the other hand a palm branch. These two objects have something in common. Can anyone guess what it is? Well then, what is a battery known for? Yes, it has power or energy. How do we get the power out of this little battery? Yes, we must connect it to something to use the life within it! It will just sit there with no particular use until we decide to connect it to something.[1] Well, this is just a branch of a palm tree and it has no particular use until we connect it with something. When it is connected to our faith it takes on a new meaning.

It has been blessed with holy water and thus is called 'sacramental', which points to something sacred. When we take this 'sacramental' and connect it to our faith it helps us connect with God, the source of our power. It is so easy to let this connection break. To let our faith just sit and do nothing. We become consumed with our ordinary daily life and find ourselves disconnected from God.

Today, I suggest that we take this palm branch and when we get home, don't just throw it on the kitchen table and forget about what we have celebrated here. If we do not choose to do something deliberate with it, then soon we will find it buried by newspapers and other stuff of our daily life. Instead, I invite all of us to place it prominently on our doors, maybe even the refrigerator door or somewhere else where we will see it every day. So every time we look upon it we will be reminded of our gift of faith.

We will be reminded of our celebration of the passion of our Lord Jesus Christ here today. We will be reminded that God became one of us and died for our sins. He came to show us the way, the truth and the life. However, we must remain connected to that message. This week we can look upon this branch and keep connected to our faith in Jesus Christ as our King and Messiah.

---

1. Adapted from concept introduced by Jim Auer, *Celebration: An Ecumenical Worship Resource*, (Kansas City, Montana: National Catholic Reporter Company, Inc., April, 2003).

Christ: Chef in the Kitchen of Life

When we go into a restaurant, who is it that serves us? The waiter or waitress, right? Maybe the busboy, host or hostess, or bartender. But who else serves us when we are eating out? Yes, of course – the cook or chef! Without them the waiter or waitress would have nothing to serve. Without them there would be no food. Without them there would be no restaurant. Yet rarely do we see the chef in the restaurant. A chef is behind everything that goes on in a restaurant, but we hardly ever see him or her. Every chef works extremely hard and serves without being seen. The only time we see the chef is when we want to complain. So it is with our lives. We seem to remember Christ only when we want to complain.

Yet like the chef in the kitchen, there would be no eternal life if it were not for Christ. Christ is behind our every breath here on earth and in eternal life.

Well, in today's gospel Jesus gives his friends an example of discipleship. He shows them, and us, what he means by service. Remember, the gospel passage is set in the Jerusalem area and at that time people wore only sandals, not shoes and socks. The roads would have been very dusty, so when people arrived into a house their feet were filthy. To wash the feet of guests was a task only for a slave or servant. If the house did not have a servant, then the youngest member of the house was obliged to wash. It was menial task, completed by the servant without much fanfare. It was certainly not a task for someone considered to be the Messiah.

Yet that is what our Lord and Master did – bend low and serve us. This was a very obvious demonstration of our need to serve one another. We are called to be servants in the background. Like the chef in the kitchen, we are called to work hard, often without being seen.

Most of us have people in our lives who serve us and yet they remain in the background. We rarely see or recognise them either for what they really do or who they really are for us, but they are really there. Maybe it is our mother or father who provide for us. Or maybe it is our grandmother or guardian. Or maybe it is our child who provides for us now that we are old or sick. Or maybe it is a friend.

Whoever it is, most of us have people who are in the background of our lives serving us. They are Christ in our lives today.

Well, today we are called to act in service to others and accept that our service may not even be seen. We are to serve others regardless of our visibility, satisfied with the grace of 'a meal well served.' We are called to put on the chef's hat of service and bend low. We are called to move to our knees and serve. It is not easy but we can do it.

We can start right now as we leave: let that other person out of the parking space first; let that other person be the first in line at the checkout; let that other person have the last word; let that other person have some of our wealth; let that other person have some of our time.

Yes, today we can serve others and be prepared to be the chefs in other people's lives, not noticed for the fine meal we produce. Today, may we act like Christ the Chef in the kitchen of life.

Judge and Saviour

There is a great story told about two people who went through college together. They were very close friends. Life went on and they went their different ways and lost contact. The first went on to become a judge, while the other went downhill and ended up a criminal. One day the criminal appeared before the judge. He had committed a crime to which he pleaded guilty. The judge recognised his old friend and faced a dilemma. He was a judge, so he had to be just; he couldn't let him off. On the other hand, he didn't want to punish his old friend because he still loved him. So he told his old friend that he would fine him the correct penalty for the offence. That is justice.

Then, the judge came down from the bench and wrote a check for the amount of the penalty. That is love.[1]

That is what God did for us in becoming human in Christ Jesus and then dying for our sins, our offences. In his justice, God judges our sinfulness because we are guilty, and in his love, he came down in the person of his Son, Christ Jesus, and paid the penalty for us too.

In this way, he is both 'just' and the one who 'loves.' He enables us to go free despite our sinfulness. He is both our Judge and our Saviour.

As the epic gospel passage shows us today, Jesus loves us so much that he was willing to die for us. In this way God makes us anew. He gives humanity a new start. We are always people in need of conversion, people in need of repentance. The process never ends.

Today of all days we ought to recognise not only the sacrifice of Christ but also the love of God through this gift to us. Now we know that death is not the end but only the beginning of new and eternal life. We will die, but we will rise.

May we be grateful for the gift of Christ today.

1. Nicky Gumbel, *Questions of Life*, (Cook Communications Ministries: Colorado Springs, Colorado, 1996) 49.

Sand to Glass:
Our Easter Journey of Transformation

Does anyone know what Silicon Dioxide (SiO2) is? It is the chemical compound for sand, ordinary sand. Yet if we take that ordinary sand and purify it by removing any traces of iron, then bleach it and add limestone and sodium carbonate, and then melt the sand by heating it to 1,700 degrees, it becomes a transparent substance we all call 'glass'. Glass that can be formed into a beautiful Cathedral stained glass window. Glass that can be formed into eyeglasses which can help someone see. Glass that can be formed into a magnificent piece of crystal.[1]

But it all starts with the ordinary sand. Sand that ceases to be sand. Sand that gives itself up to be created into something greater. Sand that is transformed into something more beautiful.

Well, I think that sand and glass is a wonderful metaphor for this Easter day. At first pass, we see the crucified Lord on Good Friday and the God-Father who is unable to protect his Son from evil. We see the ordinariness and humanity of Jesus, and see how evil seems to have conquered good.

Yet if we look deeper into this reality we see something different. Instead, we see a journey of transformation, not just for Jesus into the Risen Christ, but for all of humanity into the Body of Christ. Today is the day that we celebrate that transformation. Today is the day we recognise for sure that transformation is real. What was started at Christmas in the incarnation is complete today in the Easter resurrection. The empty tomb is the symbol of that transformation, the transformation from the sand of the desert of our lives into the crystal glass of heaven that shines brightly for all to see.

Yet that does not happen without our choosing to allow it. Tonight we welcomed 29 people into the Catholic faith, of which 15 were baptised, and all received the sacraments of initiation. They chose to be part of our church. They chose to journey through this Lent, accepting the three scrutinies and professing

---

1. *Connections* (Mediaworks, Londonderry, NH: March, 2005)

their faith in Christ. We welcome them into the transformation we call the Body of Christ.

During these last six weeks of Lent we, too, have journeyed with them through the desert sands of their lives into their final transformation. As we journeyed, we also recognised our own need for purification. We recognise the need to be purified from our sins and allow ourselves to be transformed into something new. As Paul reminds the Romans, we shall also be united with Christ in the resurrection and have newness of life. The ordinariness of the sand of our lives can be made brilliant by the transformation in Christ. We have been made new by the sacrifice of Christ and we rise with him to that transformation.

But those of us who are already Christians and Catholics must choose that journey, permitting the Lord to purify us. We need to allow the Lord to add the limestone of grace to us and be heated by the fire of the Holy Spirit. We need to allow ourselves to be transformed, from the sand of our lives into the crystal of Christ.

But there is still one more ingredient needed for the crystal or stained glass window to come alive completely. They need light to shine through them for their true beauty to come alive. So too with us, we need the light of Christ to shine through us for our true magnificence to come alive. We need to continue to allow the Lord to shine in and through us.

So as we leave here tonight and celebrate the Risen Lord, we realise that we need to allow the purification of the sands of our lives. We do this by removing any traces of sin in our lives.

Then, through the gift of the fire of the Holy Spirit and through the additive of God's grace we can, and will, be transformed into the crystal of Christ. Today may we let the light of Christ shine through us as the shining crystal of the Body of Christ and show the world that the Risen Christ is alive.

People of Hope!

Nine men were entombed in the earth for three days. They were in imminent danger of drowning in a coalmine inundated with millions of gallons of water. Their oxygen was very limited. Hypothermia was a real threat. And they had only one corned beef sandwich between them. Fearing the worst, they wrote their last words to their families on pieces of cardboard and encased them in a bucket. They prayed together and thought about their imminent death.

Above the ground an army of experts labored to rescue them, and many thought it would be a miracle if any would be found alive. Down below the men, feeling hopeless, bound and chained themselves to each other with a steel cable. They wanted to make it easier for the rescuers to locate the bodies when the drill finally broke through. Much of the world watched, waited and prayed.

After 77 hours of being entombed in a flooded mine all nine miners were rescued through a small hole drilled from the surface. Where death was feared and expected, life emerged triumphant.[1]

Well, on Holy Thursday we celebrated the Lord's last supper. There we recalled Jesus facing his own imminent death and how he gave his last words to his friends, the disciples and us, words that were not written on cardboard but given in person. Jesus told his disciples to love one another as he had loved them, and to love one another by serving each another.

Then on Good Friday we celebrated the passion of the Lord, remembering that Jesus Christ died for our sins and showed us a new way, the way of the cross. He took the sting out of death and promised us new life beyond death.

Now, on Easter Sunday, we celebrate the resurrection of Christ, moving beyond the cross to the empty tomb, showing the fullness of our salvation, converting his three days in the

---

1. Adapted from Gloria Hutchinson, *Homily Helps*, (St Anthony Messenger Press: Cincinnati, OH, April, 2003)

tomb to triumphant victory over death. And yes, we celebrate his promise of salvation for all of us.

Everyone has times when the pain of our lives seems to bury us. We become entombed by the troubles of our lives and we can feel hopeless like the miners I spoke of earlier, or like the disciples at the Last Supper. It may be the loss of a job or long-term relationship or relative, or it may be the demands of our family members or friends, or it may be something personal or professional, but whatever it is, life has a way of sometimes burying us and at times we can feel crushed.

Our first instinct is find someone to tie ourselves to. They say misery loves company. Well, we often find others who are in a similar predicament and we tie ourselves to them, wallowing in our self-pity. If others find us they will find us together, buried in our misery.

But, as Christians, we are called to a different way, the way of the cross, the way of Christ Jesus. We are called to see the hope in all things. We are called to believe in Christ, who will take us beyond the cross. We are called to love others at all costs. Like the second reading said today, we are called to be the new yeast in the lives of those around. I am not saying that it is easy! Indeed I know, and anyone who has felt the pain of life knows, it is not easy at all. But this is what we are called to be: people of hope.

Today we gather around with each other here and tie ourselves to other people of faith so we can lift each other up. So maybe we can be the one who lifts up others by being a person of faith and believing in them, even when everyone doubts them; by being people of love and loving others, even when everyone else seems to abandon them; by being people of hope and helping others to believe and love, even when everyone else seems to have given up hope.

Today and this week, indeed, this whole Easter season, may we be people of faith, love, and hope, and demonstrate by our actions that we believe in the Risen Christ.

Could It Be?

One of the things I like to do is cook. When we cook we need a couple of things, don't we? Food, yes, but even more so we need a recipe. Now, most of us will use a cookbook to find our recipes. Some of us will use a recipe from a book to start and then go from there, changing it to our tastes as we go along. Others of us will use recipes given to us by our friends whom we trust. Still others of us like to taste friends' recipes first. If we are at a friend's house enjoying a meal, we'll say, 'May I have the recipe for that?' In other words, we like to experience the food first before we try making it ourselves.

Well, in today's gospel Thomas would not take the word of his friends. He wanted to experience the Risen Christ himself: he wanted to taste the food first before he used the recipe! He said he would not believe until he could put his finger into the nail marks of Jesus' hands and his hand into Jesus' side. He would not solely believe in the words of his friends. He had to experience Jesus for himself.

In today's second reading from the Letter of John, we hear what the recipe for life is, according to Jesus. It is to obey the commandments, and to act in faith and love.

Today's gospel passage summarises it even further: to love God and to love one another. Two aspects of the same commandment – that is as simple as the recipe gets.

I think that we sometimes refuse to believe in the presence of Christ in our lives until we experience it directly for ourselves. We come to this table each week to experience the Lord anew and to be refreshed by his presence in this House of Prayer. But we are called to bring that presence of Christ to others and to see his presence in others outside of this place. Could it be that Christ is calling us to the truth of his presence already in our lives? Could it be that he is answering our prayers already? Could it be that Christ is calling us to make his presence felt at our places of work? Could it be that Christ is calling us to make his presence felt in our homes? Could it be that Christ is calling us to make his presence felt with friends and family?

Fr Liam Lawton, whom many of you know, has composed

many beautiful songs with touching lyrics. One such song is called *Could It Be?*[1] I suggest that we listen to this song now as our meditation, and ask ourselves if the Lord is calling us to see him already in our lives and to bring his recipe of life to others.

---

1. Liam Lawton, *Light the Fire*, (Chicago, IL: GIA publications, 1995) CD and book.

Way of the Philosopher – Way of the Saint

St Thomas Aquinas, the great theologian and philosopher of the 13th century, tells us that we can know a thing in two ways: the way of the philosopher and the way of the saint. The way of the philosopher is one in which we gain knowledge *about* a thing.[1] We often come to such knowledge by analysis. We break it into several parts and come know how it works. This knowledge is gained at a distance, in order to gain perspective.

The second way, the way of the saint, is different. The way of the saint is one in which we gain knowledge of a thing *for itself*. We come to such knowledge by participation in its being. This knowledge is gained not at a distance but by involvement and commitment. We exhibit reverence to allow a thing to reveal itself to us as it truly is.

All this seems very abstract and it may be helpful to think of it in another way. Fr Anthony DeMello, SJ, an Asian mystic, thought of it in more simple terms.[2] He said we gain a lot of knowledge about a rose when we dissect it; we understand its molecular makeup, how it grows, and why there are different colors. That is the way of the philosopher. But if we really want to know a rose, says DeMello, we have to experience it by smelling it, by seeing its beauty, and by allowing it to reveal itself to us. Then we truly know the rose! That is the way of the saint.

In today's second reading from the letter of John we are warned about the danger of simply knowing about God. Some in the community were claiming that they 'knew' Jesus by knowing the commandments. The implication here is that if we simply know the commandments then we know Jesus and God. However, we are told that to know God is to keep the commandments. This is something quite different.

We know lots of things about Jesus. We know where he was born and raised. We know that he performed many miracles

---

1. William F. Maestri, *Grace Upon Grace*, (Makati, Philippines: St Paul Publications, 1988) p 142
2. DeMello, Anthony SJ, *One Minute Nonsense*, (Chicago: Loyola University Press, 1992)

and said many things. We know that he was crucified, died and rose from the dead. But we only truly know Jesus when we live his commandments: love God and your neighbour as yourself.

If we are to know Christ, and God his Father, then we are to love one another as he loved us. Now, I am not an anti-intellectual or anything. The way of the philosopher is very important, but the way of the saint, according to Aquinas, is critical and maybe even essential. This is the way of holiness or the way of love. This is the way that Jesus invites us to live.

In today's gospel we are reminded of this invitation as Jesus deals with the doubting of his disciples. He tells them that they know him for who he really is because they have experienced him already. They know a lot about him, but most of all they know him for himself. Then, Jesus tells them to go and preach this to all nations.

Unfortunately, unlike the disciples in today's gospel, we do not have the luxury of experiencing Christ's presence in the flesh. However, we can and do experience Christ's presence in each other. In a special way, we experience the Body of Christ here at Eucharist when we gather around this altar to receive his Body. We become what we receive, the presence of Christ to others. And so we share this meal and ask for the strength and wisdom to be involved in others' lives and to be committed to them. By doing so, we will live Christ's commandment to go and preach the gospel.

By doing so, we will become not just philosophers, but also the saints we are all called to be.

By doing so, we will know each other for who we truly are, children of God, and saints of God.

Hearing and Listening to God's Voice

I know my sheep and my sheep know me, in the same way that the Father knows me and I know the Father.

When I was 13 years old, I used to play in the back garden of our house. When dinner was ready my mother would call from the house, 'Brendan, Brendan, dinner's ready.' If I was having too much fun I ignored her. Then she would call even louder, 'Brendan, dinner is ready; come at once.' I usually came the second time. Without even seeing my mother I recognised my mother's voice. I could even tell when she was mad at me just by the tone of her voice.

There are people in our lives whom we recognise by voice alone – our fathers, spouses, children, or best friends. But to whose voice do we listen? To whose voice do we respond?

When the gospel of John was written, most of the community for whom it was written were farmers and so the story of the good shepherd and his sheep was a very powerful illustration. Today, however, most of our lives are identified not with sheep or shepherds but with computers, television, and cellular phones. In this age of technology we easily idolise information for the sake of information, expecting it to provide our lives with meaning and to alleviate our fears. But ironically, the idol we have created soon controls us instead of freeing us.

In a world with so many voices over so many cables and computers, we wonder to whose voice we should listen. We are seduced into believing that the latest information is the answer to the meaning of our lives.

But in reality, information alone does not give us knowledge of life. Only life, truly and fully lived, can give us knowledge of life. Information can become an idol when it becomes a substitute for life.

Listening to God's voice over the plethora of voices may seem easy, but it is really hard in our busy lives. I truly believe the only way we can hear God's voice and listen to his direction is to spend some time in prayer. Only in that space do we learn to recognise his voice.

While at prayer we ought not seek a silencing of the other

voices, but rather hear God speaking through those noises. He speaks to us in the midst of this world, not away from it. God is present in the midst of the whirl winds of data. He is there. We just need to recognise his voice. We have to choose to listen and heed the sound of that voice.

In the same way, when I played and was having fun I ignored the call of my mother. Often when we are having fun, we can ignore the voice of the creator. Today we have the choice to listen.

Throughout the world on this Sunday we celebrate vocations. And so we focus on the theme of choice. Life involves choice, and we can choose to listen. If we want to be happy in our vocation of life, whether as a married, single, or religious person, then we need to listen to God's voice. We need to stop listening to the marching band of materialism, consumerism, and individualism, and challenge ourselves to listen in the midst of the surrounding noises for that one voice that calls us to him.

As children of God, Christ alone has the key to open the secret door to the meaning of our lives. And so listening to God's voice is our vocation in life.

I know my sheep and my sheep know me, in the same way that the Father knows me and I know the Father.

They Will Know We Are Christians
By Our Love

A company advertised a job opening for a salesperson and it received hundreds of applications for the position. However, out of all the resumés and letters it received one stood out above all the rest because of its honesty and its unique challenge. It stated: 'I am currently working as a salesperson in a furniture store and I am very much interested in your sales position. You ask about the quality and style of my sales skills. It is best for you to judge them for yourselves. And so I suggest you come by the store at the address below and pretend to be a customer buying some furniture. You will be able to identify me as I am tall and have red hair. I, however, will not be able to identify you. I will not be able to impress you as a future employer as I will not be able to recognise who you are. You will be able to experience me in my everyday sales approach, which will speak for itself. I look forward to seeing you anonymously!'

Intrigued by the woman's letter, the sales team took her up on the offer. Impressed not only by her confidence but by her professional and honest approach to sales, they hired her soon after.[1]

Our Christian way of life is an everyday approach. We are called to live it all day, every day and not just here on Sundays Today's scripture reminds us of the heart of the approach of this Christian way of life.

In John's first letter we hear that if we want to remain in Christ, and he in us, then we are to love one another. Yes, to be sure, Jesus' command is to love one another; he told us to love others as he loved us. Even stronger language is used in today's gospel, telling us that if we do not bear fruit then we will be pruned away. Jesus reminds us that his new way of life for the disciples is simply to love one another and serve one another. That is how we remain in his Spirit, by serving others.

Remember, this gospel section is from the gospel of John and it immediately follows the Last Supper, at which Jesus washed

---

1. Adapted from *Connections* (Mediaworks, Londonderry, NH: May, 2004)

the feet of his disciples, thus giving them an example of how to love one another. For Jesus, to love is to serve. To love others is to serve them as a way of life. To love is an everyday approach to life. There is that song we have sung for years, 'They will know that we are Christians by our love, by our love. Yes they will know we are Christians by our love.' Will they know we are Christians by 'our' love?

If Jesus had been at our dinner table last night in our homes, would he know that we love one another by the way we treated one another? If Jesus was at our last meeting at work or school, with our co-workers or students, would he know that we love one another by the way we treated one another? If Jesus was at the restaurant or store yesterday when we were served, would he know that we love one another by the way we treated the anonymous workers? If Jesus witnessed any of these interactions over this last week, from those with a close family friend to those with an anonymous stranger, would he know that we love one another?

I do not know about you but, I for one, might be a little embarrassed if Jesus were present in some of my interactions with others over this past week, month and year. If we are honest with ourselves, we come to this table not because we are so perfect, but because we need his help to live out the gospel command. We come to this table to gain strength for the rest of the week, so that we can do our best to love one another again this week. We come here each Sunday so we can recommit ourselves to our common goal – and that goal remains the same – to love one another.

We need to go back out into our daily lives and try our hardest to be Christian each day. It is an everyday thing, not just a Sunday thing. So this week as we go forth from here may we love one another in every interaction. Whether it is how we talk to our children, especially when we need to correct them. Or whether it is how we handle our parents' demands, demands of people who are now getting old and need more help in doing things. Or whether it is how we deal with our co-workers or fellow students who are pushing our limits of patience. Or whether it is how we act toward the complete stranger in the restaurant or store who is serving us in a less than ideal way.

Yes, it is how we treat each person every day that counts. If the anonymous visitor comes this week, may they know we are Christians by our love.

Love One Another

This is my commandment: love one another, as I have loved you. A person can have no greater love than to lay down one's life for one's friends.

Several weeks ago when I visited my brother and his family of three children, I remember all the children were sick. Little Sean, not even one year old, was crying up a storm and squirming all over the place. Dominic and Daniella, who are four and a half and six, were cranky and wanted to be constantly held by their mother. All of them were in need of a lot of tender loving care that night.

I stayed for the evening and went home exhausted from helping take care of them. My brother and sister-in-law continue to take care of them every day. The next day I talked with my brother and in the course of the conversation he told me that he was up most of the night with the kids again and he was completely exhausted from lack of sleep.

Not something totally uncommon for parents in those early years. But I must admit it was a reality check for me. What a total life commitment, I thought. To be on call 24 hours a day, 7 days a week. Yes, that is parenthood.

Many of you are parents and know exactly what I am talking about. And all of us should know how much our parents gave up for us. All of us were children once and I am sure we were sick at times. Our parents may have been imperfect at times, but they loved us as best they could.

Well, in today's gospel Jesus commands his disciples to love one another as he had loved them. He told them that they should be prepared to lay down their lives for one another. I cannot think of a better modern day equivalent of Christian discipleship than being a good parent. Every good parent is prepared to give up everything to ensure that their children will have what they need. They give their very lives for their children. This is most evident in those early years, but as many of you know, even as children grow and become adults, it never really stops.

The same goes for a good spouse or a good friend. Loving is

hard work! Loving is really hard work! But loving makes us more than who we are as individuals. When we love we are part of something bigger than ourselves.

In today's second reading from the first letter of John we are told that when we love one another we know God, because God *is* love. So when we love, we participate in God himself. We are actually making God real in the world. When we love our children, we are putting a face to God. We are God's hands and God's feet in this world. We are not the limit to God's love, but when we love, God's love is made real in the world. Passing on the love is part of what we do when we pass on our faith to our children.

In the first reading we are told to baptise in the name of Jesus Christ. And so in a few minutes we will baptise some children and welcome them into the church. Each of these parents will commit to raising their children in the Christian faith and loving them always. But it is not just our own children that Jesus asks us to love. Jesus asks us to love one another. Jesus asks us to love everyone in the same way that we love our children. In other words, when we see someone in need we have to ask ourselves, 'If this was my child, how could I help her or him?' That is the challenge of today's Gospel: To love everyone. To love everyone.

Now, that is very difficult, but it is what we are called to do. I believe love is the only way we will change. Love is the only way others will change. Not that we love others to change them. But by loving others we are changed and sometimes, because of our change, they want to change as well. But that project becomes their change and not ours for them.

So let us love one another and allow God to change us all.

This is my commandment: love one another, as I have loved you. A person can have no greater love than to lay down one's life for one's friends.

Finishing the Master's Work!

Puccini was the great Italian writer of classic operas such as *Madame Butterfly*. Puccini was quite young when he died of cancer. In his last days, he dedicated himself to his work, to writing his masterpiece opera, called *Turandot*. His friends would caution him, 'You're sick. Take it easy and rest.' He would always respond, 'I want to finish my last work.' Unfortunately, he died before completing his masterpiece.

But in 1926, at the famous La Scala Opera House in Milan, Puccini's opera was played for the first time. It was conducted by the famous conductor Arturo Toscanini. When it came to the part in the opera where Puccini was unable to finish because he died, Toscanini suddenly stopped. The conductor's eyes welled with tears, and turning around to the large audience he said, 'This is where the master died.' And he wept. After a few moments more, Toscanini lifted his head, smiled broadly, and said, 'And this is where his friends begin.' And he finished the opera to thunderous applause. Puccini's friends completed the masterpiece he had started.[1]

As Jesus takes leave of this world, he calls his first disciples together and asks them to finish his song.[2] He had given them a masterpiece! He showed them how to play music by living life to the fullest, and now he was asking them to show others that same gift. Jesus invited his disciples, and invites all of us, to continue the great work he started: to teach others about the Father's unlimited love for us; to teach others that we are all his children; to live as he lived while he was here on earth; and to live for others and not just for ourselves.

This 'finishing the work' is a great way to teach others. Think for a moment how we teach our children. We encourage them to express thanks for a gift by prompting them with the sentence 'what do you say now?', and allowing them to recall they are to say 'thank-you!' Or teachers in school will ask a question: 'The capital of California is ... Sacramento!' or 'The capital of England

1. William J. Bausch, *Story Telling the Word*, (Mystic, Connecticut: Twenty-Third Publications, 1996)
2. *Connections* (Mediaworks, Londonderry, NH: May, 2002)

is ... London!' Even when children play we give them colouring books and they can colour in the blanks, or jigsaw puzzles that they can fit together.

We can teach others the gospel message in this same way. We can give others a message of love and forgiveness from us and let them fill in the blanks. We start with our actions of love and let others finish the music, as Toscanini did for Puccini, by acting with love to even more people. To enable us to love and play the masterpiece Jesus gave us, his Spirit resides within us, guiding us according to his commands.

Today we can start by affirming the presence of Christ in each other and letting others continue to see Christ in us as well. Today we also celebrate Mothers' Day here in the United States, and most of us take this time as an opportunity to express our love for our mothers. Mothers have been completing the 'unfinished music' in our families, generation after generation. Maybe we can make this day a very special day for them as we acknowledge the gift of selfless giving that mothers give their families, their untiring 'finishing of the work' for us. And, as we recognise our own mothers, we are also called to 'finish the masterpiece' that Christ has started in them.

And in so doing we can start another 'unfinished opera' of Christian love in others!

We Are Sent With A Mission

There are different ways of doing something. Sometimes we do things with intention and sometimes we muddle through things without any real purpose. Our attitude makes a big difference when we set off to do something.

I remember as a child that my mother would send me to do errands. But often I would walk away and get distracted doing the task. One of the common errands was to go to the stores for some groceries. We lived right in the middle of a town and the shops were close by, only a few streets away.

On one particular occasion I remember being sent to the store as my mother called out instructions to me: 'Run up there, to the stores and get some carrots.' I wandered off with no particular hurry and on the way back took in some window-shopping. When I eventually arrived home my mom asked, 'What took you so long?' I answered casually, 'Well, I didn't know you were in a hurry and I just thought you wanted some carrots.' 'Yeah, for tonight's dinner, not next week's dinner,' my mom snapped!

There is a difference in the way we do things at times. There can be a difference in our actions when we are sent by someone to do something. When there is a sense of urgency, we ought to do the thing – act with purpose.

In today's gospel Jesus says a prayer for his disciples, that God may give them strength for the mission they are being sent to do. Christ prays that they be consecrated in the truth and that they may share in his joy. Christ then sends them on the mission to proclaim the good news to all. He sends them out with a purpose and a sense of urgency.

In the first reading from the Acts of the Apostles, Peter and the other apostles choose a successor to Judas and then also send the newly discerned Matthias on the same mission they had received from Christ.

Well, every Sunday we are sent with a mission – the mission to love one another and bring the good news to others. There is a sense of urgency about it, too. When we leave Mass, we ought to leave with a sense of purpose. We ought to leave ready to take on that mission. And so we ought to leave here with a little more joy; after all, we leave with good news for heaven's sake!

So, when someone meets us, we somehow proclaim through our words and deeds that we have been lifted up by the Spirit. It ought to be evident that our lives are being transformed, converted, and made new. We are dismissed with a purpose – to share the joy of the gospel. It's not easy work, but it is our mission.

So how do we accomplish this mission? I think the best place to start is to recognise that every single one of us has gifts, and every single one of us needs to discover our own gifts. Somehow these gifts are meant to be used for the greater good of the Body of Christ. If we use them with purpose and intention here in our community, then our actions will testify to our mission. We start here, but we do not end here. We start sharing here, but we ought to end up sharing with the greater community too.

So our mission starts in the sharing of gifts for others. Remember that there is also a sense of urgency because we ought to not take any of our gifts for granted. We need to remember that we have a limited time here on earth and we need to use our gifts as much as we can.

Today and this week may we leave this Eucharist with a real sense of purpose; may we leave here with joy in our hearts; may we leave here ready to share the good news; may we leave here with a sense of urgency to share the gifts we have; and, finally, may we leave here with a mission.

Christian Path as Our Journey of Life

In the movie *Lord of the Rings*, adapted from Tolkien's 1937 books, a god-like being named Sauron, 'lieutenant of the Prime Dark Lord,' fashioned a ring that held the power to draw together all the races of the earth and rule them under the yoke of slavery.

'One ring to rule them all.
One ring to find them.
One ring to bring them and
in the darkness bind them.'

This ring found its way to the Shire, home of the hobbits, who are friendly, good-natured, simple folk. When it is discovered that the evil Sauron knows where the ring is, he sends his armies to reclaim the ring. The good people of the world realise that the only hope is to destroy the ring before Sauron gets it, and the only way to do that is to journey to a land called Mordor, and throw the ring in the Cracks of the Mount Doom, where the ring was first made!

This difficult task falls to the unlikely Froddo, a young hobbit, and his friend Sam. Froddo's journey is not so much fated as it is chosen. Yes, he was chosen but he still had the free will to refuse the task. Instead Froddo accepts this journey, a dangerous journey, but the journey of a life time. His friend Sam goes with him on this journey, remaining loyal to the last day, even carrying him when Froddo is unable to continue.

Sam accompanies Froddo out of love and friendship. Froddo did not know what was ahead of him, but he still chose to follow the unknown path, committed to the journey ahead.

While Tolkien refused any allegorical reading into his books, he conceded that his stories are laden with the Christian narrative. Namely, hidden in the story of the 'Lord of the Rings' is the story of every Christian, the journey we all must go on.[1]

Today we celebrate the beginning of the universal church with the Feast of the Pentecost – the giving of the gift of the Holy Spirit to the disciples. We celebrate not so much the beginning of

---

1. Andrew Krivak, 'Author of 'The Rings': Tolkien's Catholic Journey,' in *Commonweal*, (New York, December 19, 2003) p 12

an institution, whether local or universal, but more the beginning of a journey of the People of God, as the people chosen to bring the good news to all nations, to bring all people everywhere into the knowledge of God's love. We celebrate the beginning of a journey for all of us. Yes, we recognise in our community what we have done and what God has done, what we are doing and what God is doing but even more, we recognise what we will do and what God will do through us. Like Froddo in the 'Lord of the Rings,' we do not know what is ahead of us on this unknown path of life as a Christian, but we choose it freely.

But we are not alone on this journey. The Lord promises to be with us always and so he sends the gift of the Holy Spirit to remain loyal to us. Like Sam accompanying Froddo for their entire odyssey, so too does the Holy Spirit accompany us for our entire life's journey. No matter where we go, the Spirit of God will be with us; no matter what we do, the Spirit of God will be there.

God sends that gift to us as individuals, and as a community of believers, so that we can know that we are the same Body of Christ, diverse in gifts, but one body!

None of us knows what is ahead of us this week, good or bad, yet we are called to follow the unknown path ahead. As Christians we come to this table each week to receive nourishment for the journey of the week ahead. We do not claim to know what is ahead but in faith we accept all as a gift from God to see his presence.

If we are honest, we know we need this nourishment from the table of the Lord each and every week, because living a Christian life is not easy. Sometimes we feel like Froddo, who loses hope at several points on the journey, and we want to quit this seemingly endless and treacherous task. We, too, tire of, and lose hope of, being Christian to others

  – to love others when they will not love us in return;
  – to forgive others when they will not forgive us in return;
  – to visit and spend time with others
  when they will not acknowledge our presence.

No, being on the Christian path of life is not easy at all and we come to this table for food for the journey. We need to see each other as co-pilgrims on life's journey and recognise in each other the need for assurances in faith.

So today as we leave here and recognise the gift of the universal church, as well as the gift of our local church, know also that Christ has sent his gift from the Father, the Holy Spirit, to be with us on our journey of life. He will be with us always until the end of time. We do not know what will be ahead of us this week but we chose the Christian path as our journey of life.

What Are You Listening For?

A Native American was in downtown New York walking along with his friend, who lived in New York City. Suddenly he stopped and said, 'I hear a cricket.' 'Oh, you're crazy,' his friend replied. 'No, I am serious and I really do! I am sure of it.' His friend said, 'It's noon in New York City. The people are bustling around, cars honking, taxis squealing and you say you hear a little cricket. I don't think so!' But the Native American persisted, 'I'm absolutely sure.' And he started to search for the little creature. He walked down the street to the corner and there he found a little shrub in a large cement planter. He dug behind the leaves and there was the cricket!

His friend was duly astounded and said, 'Wow, that's impressive hearing!' But the Native American replied, 'No. My ears are no different from yours. It simply depends on what you are listening to. Here let me show you.'

He reached into his pocket and pulled out a handful of coins – a few quarters, some dimes, nickels and pennies. And he dropped them on the concrete. Every head within twenty feet turned and looked. 'You see what I mean!' said the Native American as he picked up the coins. It all depends what you are listening for.'

I think the same can be said of our relationship with God. Sometimes we complain we cannot hear him. Sometimes we say that God does not seem to be present to us. In reality it depends on what we are listening for. It depends on how aware we are of his presence in our life. It depends if we are listening to the soft sounds of the 'cricket of the Holy Spirit' within us. I believe we can attune ourselves to that sound!

In today's first reading from Deuteronomy we hear Moses give his farewell address to the people of Israel, as they prepare to cross the Jordan River into the Promised Land. He warns them not to make the same mistake as their ancestors and forget that they are a people chosen by God. He warns them to always remember to be grateful to God for the many gifts that God gives them. They are not to think of themselves as self-sufficient but they are to rely on the grace of God for all things.

In the second reading we hear Paul tell the Romans, and us,

that we ought to remember that we are adopted children of God. We received the Spirit so that we can realise that we are God's children and know how much God cares for us. That same Spirit dwells within us. But we have to believe that message – the Holy Spirit lives within us. Yes, we are the Temple of the Holy Spirit. And so we can call God, 'Abba', 'Father.'

The Father gave us his Son so that we could experience a taste of heaven. Christ gave us the Holy Spirit as a gift from the Father so that we can live always in him, as children of the Father.

Therefore we are called to attune our minds to the voice of the Holy Spirit and listen for his soft whispers in the midst of busyness. Like the Native American capable of hearing the cricket in the midst of a busy New York City, we, too, are capable of hearing God's voice in the midst of our busyness. But we must attune ourselves to the sound of his voice. And that takes practice!

This week we can practise listening. In our hectic lives today it seems that we are easily distracted by other sounds. Perhaps it is not the jingle of money that distracts us, but maybe it is the amassing of other material goods beyond our needs, such as a second house or car. Or maybe it is the grabbing for positions of power at work. Or maybe it is the gossip about other people's lives!

And distractions are not just negative. There are many positive distractions, such as caring for our children or our elderly parents, or working two jobs to keep up payments on a home for our family, or working all day and evening to keep up with school assignments. There are many real distractions and much busyness in our lives.

However, we are called to hear the 'cricket' in the midst of the busyness. It is easy to hear God's voice at the Eucharist like this, but it is out in the real world that we are called to live the gospel. It is out in the real world that we are called to preach to all nations.

May we promise ourselves this week to listen carefully to the sound of the Holy Spirit 'cricket' within us and let it guide us to where God wants us to go.

Giving Life to Others

In the world we live in today, blood transfusions are a matter of medical routine. Indeed, many of us give blood to the Red Cross on a regular schedule, to help maintain an ongoing supply. Some of us may respond at blood drives, or in times of emergency, such as after September 11th a few years ago. For our hospitals and medical laboratories, giving and receiving of blood is routine. However, it was not always that way.

Not so long ago if a person lost a lot of blood, he or she died. There were no transfusions and no blood donations. We know that if we have no blood then we have no life. From ancient times people understood blood as life itself. They understood that to give blood away is to give your life itself away. The Israelites had the same understanding instinctively. Blood meant life. The use of blood was a sign of great significance.

Indeed a contract or covenant between two parties would use the blood of an animal to seal the deal.[1] In some cultures, a covenant or contract was sealed by human blood, with a bloody thumbprint adding even greater significance.

In today's first reading from the book of Exodus we hear about one such covenant at Mount Sinai. With this new covenant between God and his people, Moses sprinkled animal blood on the table and on the people, sealing the covenant with God. By virtue of the blood used as powerful witness, Israel was now bound to God, and God to Israel, as family. Despite the people's failure to live up to this covenant, God never gave up on the people or the covenant. He always remained faithful.

In today's second reading, the author of the Letter to the Hebrews re-appropriates the Sinai covenant in light of Christ Jesus. The old covenant sealed by the blood of goats and bulls is replaced by the new covenant sealed by the blood of Christ Jesus. This is the most powerful message yet! He is an unblemished lamb to be sacrificed at the table. He is the Lamb of God. He gives of himself willingly.

1. Patricia Datchuck Sanchez, *Celebration: An Ecumenical Worship Resource*, (Kansas City, Montana: National Catholic Reporter Company, Inc. June 22, 2003)

As the gospel of Mark puts it in today's passage, 'This is my blood, the blood of the covenant, to be poured out on behalf of many.' This promised covenant was eternal, written now on the hearts of the people. Through Jesus this covenant was extended to all nations and peoples everywhere. And we are invited into that same covenant sealed by the blood of Christ.

Today we celebrate the Solemnity of the Body and Blood of Christ. In the past, this was called Corpus Christi (Body of Christ) but was renamed to more accurately tell us what we celebrate. We celebrate not only the presence of Christ in the bread, but also the presence of Christ in the wine. We are reminded explicitly today of what we celebrate at every Mass: that Christ gave his very life, his blood, for us and for all.

Sometimes the celebration of this becomes rote. We come and go to Sunday Eucharist not realising the profound reality of the facts. Jesus Christ, the Son of God, gave his life, his very blood so that we could have new life in him. If we reflect on it, we must come to acknowledge that we rely on Christ's life flowing within us.

And each time we celebrate the Eucharist, we seal again that covenant to which we recommit our lives. We promise to try again to live by that covenant this week. When we receive the Body and Blood of Christ today, remember we are committing to becoming what we receive, the Body of Christ shared for others and the Blood of Christ poured out for others.

But do we really commit? Christ gives us life by his living presence within us. So we are called to give life to others by our presence. When we are with others we are called to give life to them. Instead of being the one who tears down, we are called to build up. Instead of seeing only the negative in people, we are called to see the positive values. Instead of complaining of the bad things that happen to us, we are called to focus on the good things that occur.

Yes, we are called to be the one who lifts people's spirits. We are called to be the one who brings life to conversation, and who brings life to others by our presence. Today and this week may we be life givers to others and so bring the Blood of Christ to life in others.

Brick By Brick

As is the case in many families, Mom was the caregiver to their little daughter Mollie. A bruise or cut was tended to by Mom, a question raised by something overheard at school would be saved for Mom, and the bedtime ritual of brushing teeth, prayer and story would be presided over by Mom.

Dad had a very different relationship with Mollie. Their time together centred around goal-oriented things, such as learning to swim or ride a bike. Dad sometimes worried that his time did not matter as much as Mom's. The turning point came one summer evening.

Mollie was in the backyard trying to build a 'secret hideout' out of large cardboard pieces that kept toppling over. For days she and her friends tried to keep the walls up, but they would fall at the slightest breeze. Mollie was frustrated to the point of tears. 'You know what you need to make this, Mollie?' Dad says. 'What?' 'You need about 60 bricks.' 'Yes, but where can we get 60 bricks.' 'The hardware store. Get your shoes on and hop in the truck.' So Dad and Mollie went to the hardware store and bought the bricks they needed.

When they got home and Dad started to unload the bricks from the truck, Mollie begged, 'Oh, please, let me do that, Dad. Please!' 'But, Sweetie, they're really heavy.' 'Please! I really want to do it myself.' So Mollie picked up a brick and carried it to the pile. Back and forth to the truck she went, one brick at a time. Dad thought to himself, 'This is going to take all night,' but he didn't mind because she seemed to be enjoying it. It was rare for them to spend time alone together.

As they worked together, Mollie became chatty, talking about what she would build with the bricks, about school and her friends there, about her horseback lessons and other parts of her life. For the first time, Dad was fully present to Mollie. Mollie did not want her Dad for what he could give her or where he could take her. She wanted Dad for Dad's sake! Ironically, in buying bricks to build a wall, Mollie and her Dad were actually tearing down a wall ... brick by brick.[1]

---

1. *Connections*, (Mediaworks, Londonderry, NH: June, 2005)

It is often the simplest things that can give us the most satisfaction in life. It is in the simplest things in life that Christ calls us to be most fully present. It is in the simplest things in life that our call to discipleship is made real.

In today's gospel we hear how the disciples are curious about Jesus. They did the simplest thing in following after this mysterious and powerful man named Jesus. They did the simplest thing in listening and learning from Jesus. They did the simplest thing in wanting to be with Jesus.

Jesus' invitation to 'Come and see' is a masterpiece of John's gospel. To come to Jesus meant to have faith in him. To see Jesus meant to perceive him with the eyes of faith. The disciples, and we, as we listen today, are called to come to Jesus and have faith in him. We are called to see Jesus and perceive him with eyes of faith.

This process of faith is like building a wall brick by brick. It requires us to spend some time with the Lord and learn his ways so we can see his hand at work. We spend this time with God chatting to him about our days at work with our colleagues, chatting about our friends at school, chatting about our challenges and joys of home life – in fact, we chat about any aspect of our lives.

We can build this wall of faith a brick at a time if only we are willing to come and see the Lord at work in our lives. We can also make known the presence of God in others' lives, by our willingness to sit and chat with others, to share their days.

Today the scripture readings challenge us to our vocational call to follow God. We do this by being ready to spend some time with God in prayer and by being ready to spend some time with others.

It is in the simplest things that we live as people of faith brick by brick.

Taking the Time to do it Right!

During the week, one of my friends was wearing a company sweater with a project slogan on it stating how committed his company is to excellence in research and development. It read, 'Making the time to do it right.' What a great slogan!

I mean, as Christians, we ought to adopt that slogan as our own. Making the time to do it right! Making the time to do the right thing in our lives always.

Certainly in today's readings from scripture we are reminded of the urgency of time. In the first reading we hear how Jonah preached to the Ninevites about the judgement of God and their need to repent. In the letter to the Corinthians Paul preaches about how time is passing away and how the time we have is short. Then in the gospel we hear Jesus himself proclaim the good news, 'This is the time of fulfillment. The kingdom of God is at hand. Repent, and believe in the gospel.'

Time is definitely one connection woven through today's readings. What is interesting is that the different groups of people reacted the same way when they heard the message of repentance. Their reaction was immediate. Not tomorrow, not next week or next year, but immediate. When the Ninevites heard Jonah's proclamation of God's wrath, they really heard, and heeded, the message. They immediately declared a fast and repentance for all citizens. They repented and turned back to God. When the Gentiles heard Paul, they immediately turned away from sin and back to God. Finally, in the gospel we hear how the first disciples reacted to their call. They acted immediately by following the Lord. They didn't say, 'Oh let's have dinner and talk about this!' No, they immediately followed by dropping their fishing nets and following him.

We, too, are called to follow the Lord immediately. Not tomorrow, not next week ... but right now! Right now at this table of the Lord. When we come to the church we are following the Lord and we are nourished by his presence here among us. But we are called to follow the Lord outside these walls too.

This week we celebrate Catholic Schools Week and we recognise all those who dedicate themselves to the education of our children. They make the world of difference in our children's lives, and we are called to make a world of difference in each other's lives, too.

But we must be prepared to use our time wisely. We need to make the time to pray and do the right things. If we do not make the time to pray, prayer will not miraculously happen on its own.

Many of you who are retired have shared with me how time seems to fly, even though you have very little scheduled to do in any one day! For most of us, prayer does not just happen; we need to decide to do it. We must be willing to make the time to do it right. When we use time well, we can do so

Perhaps this week we can make the time to pray. Maybe we can make time to spend with our family, to spend it with our children, and with our parents, who desperately need our love and time. This week we can, and we ought to, make the time.

We must make the time to do the right thing!

Listening with Attentiveness

I have a friend who is a principal of an elementary school and she always speaks of this one teacher. She is impressed by his teaching methods for a number of reasons but primarily because the children really learn from him. 'His greatest achievement is his classroom management,' she maintains. 'The children really listen and do what he says. When he speaks, they listen with attentiveness. When he asks, they obey with eagerness. He teaches with great authority and effectiveness.'

Of course, at the beginning of the school year they do not start out like that, but the children learn to listen and obey his every instruction. For the first two weeks, the teacher sets the limits for behaviours and when the students cross the boundaries they are warned. The teacher has a simple two-step process, verbal and action. If a child misbehaves, he asks the student to stop this disruptive behaviour and explains the limited choices that student now has. Then, if the child acts up again, he moves to the action step, following through with a time-out if needed.

Through this simple two-step process he teaches with great authority and helps his students learn and grow in knowledge. All the children know that if they obey then they will learn together. But they also know that if they misbehave then they will be given a time-out.

The critical thing about this teacher is that he only addresses the one student who is misbehaving and not the whole class. Furthermore, he never shames the student in any way, but calls that student to reform his/her behaviour, learning to grow in knowledge. He identifies with exactness the student's behaviour that is at issue and not the student himself.

In today's gospel Jesus speaks with great authority and everyone in the synagogue listens with attentiveness. When one person, who is possessed by an evil demon, attempts to disrupt the teaching, Jesus simply commands the unclean spirit to leave him. Just like the school teacher in my example earlier, Jesus approaches the one person who is struggling with a demon, and instead of addressing the whole person as evil, he only addresses the evil within the person.

So it is also true with us, Jesus sees the goodness that we do and we are. But he also sees the darkness within us that is blocking that goodness. He does not judge us as a whole person but rather calls us to reform and move back toward him. Jesus brings us to a place in our lives where we can see our actions and behaviours that cause us to block our growing in the Spirit.

Jesus comes into the world to free us from evil and to inform us that we have the power, through his grace, to overcome it. But we must choose it. We need to listen to his commands and be ready to obey. Jesus' way of teaching then calls us to listen with attentiveness and obey with eagerness.

When we begin our discipleship we do not always listen so well, and we often choose to follow our own ways in life contrary to his way. But Jesus also follows a two-step process. He asks us, through the scriptures, to stop our misbehaviour, and warns us we have a choice in the future. He wants us to reform our lives and turn toward the gospel. If we follow his commands, then we will learn and grow in the spiritual life and attain eternal life in heaven.

If, however, we do not listen, then we will put ourselves outside of his joy-filled way of life. But just like the schoolteacher at my friend's school, Jesus never gives up on us and constantly calls us to reform.

This week may we listen with attentiveness and obey with eagerness the call of Christ, and reform our lives to his commands. May we follow the teaching authority of Christ.

Service With A Smile!

Several years ago when I was sick and in hospital, I remember praying to God to heal me. I remember pleading with him that if he healed me I would do this and that – listing the things I would promise to do. Have any of you ever done that when you were sick? Have you ever bargained with God?

As I think back on it, the miracle was not so much the physical healing, although that was a miracle in itself, but the real miracle for me was the grace to follow through on the things that I had promised to do. I mean, God gave me the courage and the strength to follow through on some very difficult challenges.

In today's gospel we hear one of the shortest miracle stories in the Bible, the evangelist Mark's rendition of the healing of Simon's mother-in-law. We hear how Simon-Peter tells Jesus that his mother is sick, then Jesus goes to her and raises her up and she is healed. Although the curing of her physical illness was important, the real miracle is about what happens after she is cured. She immediately starts to serve others!

At first this seems jarring. Then we realise that Evangelist Mark is telling us something about how God operates in the world. When we are touched in some way by Jesus Christ, we follow a path of conversion and, walking this path, we feel compelled to serve others. The miracle, if you would, is what happens after we hear about Jesus.

As St Paul puts it in today's second reading, he is compelled to preach the gospel always. So we are compelled to preach the gospel in our actions. When Simon's mother-in-law is cured, as Mark tells us in the reading, she immediately begins to 'wait' or 'serve'; the Hebrew word for wait or serve is similar to the root word for 'disciple '. In other words, she immediately becomes a disciple. For to be a disciple is to serve others.

So we are called to be open to conversion and act as a disciple. It seems that many of us are already in serving roles. For example, you who are parents, is it not true that you spend most of your time serving the needs of your children? Or some of you may take care of older parents or your in-laws. Possibly, your job is one of service to others.

Yes, it is true that many of us are already in service roles. And these roles can be very exhausting, seeming without end. If we could only see that these actions are indeed our discipleship. It is the way we follow Jesus in our own lives.

St Thérèse of Lisieux has a beautiful way of putting it: 'Our Lord does not so much look at the greatness of our actions, nor even at the difficulty of our actions, but at the love with which we do the actions.'

It seems to me that often we perform these serving actions reluctantly, whether we are serving our children, parents, siblings or even friends. Yes, we serve them, but we sometimes do it begrudgingly. Remember we are called instead to follow the example of Simon's mother-in-law. We are called to serve out of gratitude. We ought to be thankful that we are healthy enough to be able to serve.

When we come to this table each Sunday we offer thanks to God. Today, maybe we can offer thanks to God for our health, for the fact that we are able to serve. So we are compelled as Christians to serve others with joy in our hearts. There is that company motto: 'Service with a smile.' Maybe we ought to listen to those words, and serve each other not only with a smile on our lips but also in our hearts, aware that we are blessed to be healthy enough to serve.

And if we are sick and praying for healing, let us pray not only for our own healing, but also for the strength to serve others.

This week may we take the miracle story of Simon's mother to heart. May we realise that our service to each other is our discipleship. But it is not just performing the service; rather, it is the way in which we serve. Today and this week, may we be ready to give service with a smile.

Reach Out and Touch

On their famous expedition across the United States, Lewis and Clark made history because of their bravery and discoveries. Accompanying them on that journey was another young man. This man travelled with them throughout the entire journey, and on several occasions risked his life for them. He was William Clark's black slave – York.

Halfway through the trip York's life would change forever. A stay with the Mandan Indians in the Dakotas changed his view of life. The Mandans were amazed by York's black skin, as they had never seen a black person before. They believed he must be a god of some sort and lavished him with countless favors. They touched his skin with great reverence, and treated him better than Lewis or Clark. York, as a slave, had only known hardship and disfavour. Now, with the Mandan attention and touch, he believed for the first time in his life that he had value and dignity.

Despite York's newfound respect from the Mandans, William Clark could not bring himself to free this faithful servant. Indeed, hearing of the incident, Thomas Jefferson could not bring himself to free the slave either.[1]

In today's gospel we hear how a leper comes to Jesus for healing. Jesus could have chosen simply to say to the leper, 'You are healed.' He had healed this way before. But instead, he reached out and touched the 'unclean' man. As the reading today shows, Mark is very concise with his words, and he writes no word without a reason.

In this passage, Mark the evangelist wants us to understand that Jesus reaches out to the afflicted, to touch the untouchable. He heals those whom others don't even want to see. He turns their laws upside down, intentionally.

Jesus heals the man by first touching him. It seems to me that we have many lepers in our society today, and maybe even in our own lives, too. I do not mean lepers in the physical way, as those with Hansen's disease or other skin diseases. But rather I

---

1. *Homily Helps*, (St Anthony Messenger Press: Cincinnati, OH, February, 2003)

mean lepers in the spiritual, emotional, or mental way – those people we keep on the outside of our circle of friends or family – or those people we choose to ignore or keep at a distance, for some reason. Maybe it is our difficult neighbour, or an unpopular classmate; perhaps it is an annoying co-worker, or demanding in-law. We are only willing to take these people back into our lives if and when they change. In other words, we are saying to them, 'heal yourself first and then I will love you.'

However, in the second letter today we are reminded by St Paul that we are called to imitate Christ in all things. Therefore, we are called to touch these people first. We are called to love them despite their ugliness. We are called to love first. I do not believe we all have the miraculous powers of healing, but I believe strongly that if we stretch out and touch those whom we most dislike, or even hate, we will find healing and so will they.

Yes, we are called to first touch, and then healing will happen. This week, can we treat others like the Mandans treated the black slave York? They reached out and touched him with great reverence! Can we reach out and touch like Jesus did, and bring healing to those who most need it?

Who is the leper in our life? Is it the difficult neighbour who never wants to greet us, or the unpopular classmate who never agrees with anyone, or the annoying co-worker who has his own way of doing things, or the demanding in-law who manages to burrow under our skin? Or maybe it is someone of a different faith or someone from a different race or culture.

This week, may we identify the lepers in our lives, and reach out and touch them first so God can heal them.

Active Players in the Game of Life

When I was growing up in Ireland I played Rugby competitively and enjoyed it immensely. For those of you who do not know Rugby, it is like American Football but without the pads or protection, and the ball cannot be passed forward but may only be passed laterally.

I loved those days of intense competition when my body was young! Anyway, I remember we had avid, enthusiastic supporters who would attend our every game. After each game we would have a line of people telling us how we could have played better!

I remember one man in particular who was a big personal supporter, and after the game he would list the analysis of every single play. At first, it seemed helpful and even enlightening, but then it became burdensome, as his advice was unrealistic. Soon he was impossible! So I wondered to myself how long it was since he played the game himself.

After some investigation I discovered that not only was it a long time since he played, but in fact he had never played at all. He had neither played nor coached. He had never once ventured the sport himself. You see, he was a sideline player!

In today's gospel we hear how different characters relate to Jesus. There were the sideline players of the Pharisees and scribes, who judged the actions of others, criticising their every move. Indeed, they judged the actions of the main player, Jesus, telling him how he could have done it better.

But then there were the active players, those who acted in faith and played the game of life with hope and trust in Jesus. They were the four young men, friends who carried their paralytic friend on a mat and through the roof, placing him before Jesus. You see, they took the risk and played! They acted out of their belief in Jesus Christ, that he was the healer of illnesses and forgiver of sins. They played the game of life with faith.

We, too, are called to play the game of life with faith in Jesus Christ. We are invited to put on the Christian garments of faith at baptism and play our part as people who believe in the God who saves. We are called to be active players in the game of life – except, this game is for real!

There are times when we need to be carried to the feet of Jesus because our faith is weak and our lives are in a mess. Most of us have experienced such difficult times. It is then that we rely on our friends, our family, and our community to carry us through and reinforce our faltering faith.

There are other moments when we are called to carry our friends, our family, and other community members when their faith is weakened.

How clever the paralysed man's friends were![1] They figured out a way to get him to Jesus. We might pray for the same ingenuity at this Eucharist. We know of so many people with physical illness and others with internal needs, all of whom want to be healed and forgiven.

The story today reminds us that Jesus wants to heal us, but it also reminds us of the need for human involvement in getting those in need to Jesus. The paralysed man would not have been healed if his believing friends hadn't gotten involved.

We will need ingenuity and wisdom to know what our role in the healing of others will be. When shall we speak up, or hold our tongues? When should we do something, or when should we wait? We are called not to be sideline commentators, but to be active players in the Christian life.

---

1. Jude Siciliano, OP, *Preachers Exchange*, (Raleigh, NC: preachex@op-south.org)

New Beginnings

No one pours new wine into old wineskins ...
Rather, new wine is poured into fresh wineskins.

As part of my ministry here at our parish, I am involved in marriage preparation. This involves meeting with each engaged couple several times to discuss their upcoming marriage. Fundamentally, my role is the sacramental preparation – connecting the sacrament itself to their future lives together. It is a real gift for me to be a part of these young couples' lives during this time.

Indeed, one special part of this ministry is when the couples share their dreams and hopes for their new beginning together. Invariably, they balance their hopes and dreams with their concern about their need to change and to adapt to their new life together. They are like new wine when they get married and thus require some new wineskins to hold their marriage together.

This process of becoming new wine and being new wineskins for each other mirrors the Christian journey. It is a new beginning that requires the shedding of the past and embracing of the future!

Many people present here today are married. Maybe you can remember when you got married. At the new beginning of your life together, what did you have to do differently than you did before? What past habits or possessions did you both have to shed? What new future did you embrace together?

And for those of us who are not married, perhaps when we started at a new school or a new job, we had to do something differently. What past habits or possessions did we have to shed? What new future did we embrace?

As Christians, we are constantly called to shed the past and embrace something new in the future, though in different ways. Indeed, we are called to shed our sinfulness and start life anew. This is not a once-only occasion at baptism, but rather it is a constant series of repeated steps on the journey of life. We are called to shed our sinful ways each moment of the daily journey. Each time we sin or make mistakes we are called to repent and start over.

Today's readings are full of proclamations of new beginnings, and the metaphor of marriage is used in the first reading and in the gospel. In the first reading, the prophet Hosea reminds the people of the Israel that God has taken them for his spouse and loves them as a wife, despite their infidelity. He calls them to shed their unfaithful past and join him anew in his relationship, 'in marriage'.

And in the gospel of Mark, Jesus compares himself to being a bridegroom married to us, the people of God, his church. He calls us his new Bride and pledges his love to us. He tells us there is a new beginning in him and it is not restricted to the Old Covenant. He gives us this New Covenant, in the Spirit, and this New Covenant involves his life, death and resurrection.

That is the very thing we do when we come here together each Sunday at Eucharist – we celebrate his paschal mystery as community. We thank God for the gift by sharing in his body and blood and, in so doing, we all renew our relationship as part of the Bride of Christ, his church.

But in the second reading from Corinthians, St Paul goes even further and tells us that this new beginning, already begun in Christ, must bear fruit in our lives by how we live. We must become our own letter of recommendation. People must see in us the best of what we claim to be. Put another way, others should know that we are Christians by our actions. People must see Christ and be willing to shed the past and embrace the future. As you know, we often fail to live up to this expectation.

And so, to be successful in this endeavor of living as Christians, we must examine our actions over the last day, week or month. As we begin our Lenten journey, it is a good time to reflect on our need to change certain things in our past and shed something old. We must examine our need to embrace the future with new hopes or dreams. We are called to become new wineskins, allowing room for the new wine of Christ. It requires of us a new beginning and a shedding of the past and embracing of the future.

In faith, we can move beyond the past by acknowledging it and asking for forgiveness. In hope, we can embrace our future with Christ and in love we can live in the present by being Christ to one another.

No one pours new wine into old wineskins ...
Rather, new wine is poured into fresh wineskins.

Spirit of the Law

An elderly couple went to their pastor asking him to marry them in the church. Inquiring into their situation, he discovered that they were already married over 45 years earlier, but not in the church. When they got married back 45 years ago, they both had been married before. One marriage ended in divorce and the other ended by the death of the spouse. Even though they had wanted to get married in the church, back then they were not allowed to do so until an annulment was granted.

Because the husband did not want to put his former wife through that ordeal, the new couple got married outside the church. Now, after all these years, his former wife had died and they could marry without impediment. All those years, they had never failed to attend church weekly, although they declined to receive communion.

Imagine: they had starved themselves of spiritual nourishment for all those years.

After listening to their story, the pastor informed them that the marriage preparation process would be six months long and they would have to attend a Marriage Preparation course held every Monday night for six weeks. After the Marriage Preparation classes, they would have to meet with him for four sessions to learn about the Sacrament of Matrimony.

The couple pleaded with the pastor to shorten the preparation, stating that they had been married already for 45 years, longer than the priest was alive. Besides, they only wanted a simple wedding with no fanfare. But the pastor would not relent, stating that the local church law requires that every couple take the marriage preparation as stated.

And the couple left broken-hearted, for they were both elderly and uncertain how much time and good health they had left.

Upon the insistence of one of their friends, the couple went to their neighbouring parish and met with another pastor. After explaining their story again, the new pastor gladly agreed to do the wedding that very day. After signing all the necessary papers, they celebrated the Sacrament of Matrimony in the midst of Sacrament of Eucharist and received communion at the table for the first time in 45 years. What a joyous day it was for the elderly couple as they received communion with tears flowing down their faces!

Which of the two pastors do you think understood the law? Was it the young pastor, who applied the law as he had learned it, or the other pastor who took a pastoral approach to the elderly couple? Of course, it is a rhetorical question, for who in their right mind would have refused the couple their wedding day after waiting forty-five years!

In today's gospel, Jesus and his disciples are not obeying the law of the Sabbath *per se*, not as it was handed down through the tradition. The Pharisees were quick to complain and challenge Jesus when his disciples were picking corn from the fields to eat, and even more so when he cured the man with the withered hand.

But Jesus asks the Pharisees in return, 'Is it lawful to do good on the Sabbath rather than to do evil, to save life rather than to destroy it?' They remained silent and in so doing condemned themselves.They were keeping to the letter of the law, but had missed the Spirit of the law.

The Pharisees constantly added further burdens on the people, one after another, and never lifted a finger to help them to live the law. And Jesus got angry with their rigid application of the law. They had missed the spirit of the law and how God calls us to live by loving one another.

Jesus tells us that the Spirit of the law is more important than the law itself. 'The Sabbath was made for man, and not man for Sabbath.' We are called to remain faithful to the law at all times, but if it goes against love, then we need to re-examine the application. We don't want to be like the young pastor who applies the letter of the law, and thereby miss its point.

Rather, we should strive to be like the other pastor who applied the law with love and welcomed the elderly couple to the table with the Lord again. We, too, are called to live the Spirit of the law when dealing with each other. Yes, we are called to live the letter of the law but we are also called to apply it pastorally for every situation.

Today, when we are dealing with our children, parents, friends or enemies may we apply the law with a pastoral approach, ensuring that the Spirit of the law is lived first.

You Are My Brother or Sister

The nurse escorted a tired, anxious young man to the bedside of an elderly patient. 'Your son is here,' the nurse whispered into the ear of the dying man. She had to repeat the words several times before his tired eyes opened. The man was heavily sedated and he struggled to breathe through the oxygen clip. He could barely see the young man standing beside his bed; he simply reached out his hand and the young man tightly wrapped his fingers around it, squeezing it with tenderness and assurance.

The nurse brought a chair for the young man. For the rest of the night he sat by the old man's bed, holding his hand and gently stroking his forehead. The old man said nothing.

As dawn broke, the old man died. The young man gently released the lifeless hand he had been holding all night and went to notify the nurse.

The young man waited until the nurse completed the necessary tasks. The nurse began to offer the young man her condolences, but he interrupted her. 'Who was that man?' he asked the nurse. The startled nurse said, 'I thought he was your father.' 'No, he wasn't. I never saw him before tonight.' 'Then why didn't you say something when I took you to him?' The young man said quietly, 'I knew he needed his son, and obviously his son wasn't here. My own father just died, and I understand what he and his son must have been going through. When I realised he was too sick to tell whether or not I was his son, I knew how much he needed me for those last few hours.'[1]

The kingdom of God that Jesus refers to transcends labels, stereotypes and traditions. In God's eyes, we are all his children. In God's heart, we are all brothers and sisters to one another. The young man in the story embraced that vision of Christ, and acted as the 'son' to the old, dying man.

We all have a choice in how we act each day, and we can choose to act according to God's vision. The issue is that making such choices is not so easy to do.

In the first reading from the Book of Genesis, we hear how Adam was influenced by Eve in committing evil, and how Eve, in turn, was influenced by the serpent. The story of the first fall

---

1. *Connections*, (Mediaworks, Londonderry, NH: February, 2005)

of humanity testifies to the fact that we, human beings, were created by God as free agents. We are capable of good and glorious acts and yet we are also capable of evil and wicked acts. The choice is ours.

But if we are honest we will acknowledge that we are easily influenced by others in our decisions. We often listen to the serpent in our lives and turn away from God. However, no matter what choice we make, God never abandons us and he will keep searching for us. 'Where are you?' he calls.

When we meet our God face to face and see the truth of the matter, we are given the grace to turn back again. But again, that choice is ours. We have the choice to do good or to do evil (or fail to do good.) When we do good, we will often be dismissed as crazy or a show-off. We will be easily misunderstood for our actions or motives. When we tend to the needs of those dying from AIDS, or to the homeless, we will be called foolhardy or plain crazy. When we give generously to charity, people will be suspicious of us, claiming we are seeking a tax break or seeking publicity. When we dare to challenge the *status quo*, we will be called troublemakers and receive scorn from those in authority.

Yet that is what Jesus did in today's gospel. He proclaimed the nearness of the kingdom of God, and his contemporaries thought he was crazy. He tended to the needs of the sick and lonely. He welcomed strangers, and those who were imprisoned. He proclaimed the good news of God to all.

Today and this week, may we open our eyes to the needs of others and choose to act according to God's vision.

May we treat others as our brothers and sisters.

Potential Within

One day a partially deaf boy came home from school with a note. The note told the boy's parents to take the boy out of school because he was 'too stupid to learn'. When the boy's mother read the note, she said, 'My son Tom is not "too stupid to learn". I'll teach him myself.'

When Tom died many years later, the people of the United States paid him a tribute. For one full minute they turned off the nation's lights. That man was Thomas Edison and he invented the light bulb. He also invented the motion picture, as we know it and recorded music, as we know it. He had thousands of patents in his name.

The history books are full of stories of gifted people whose talents were overlooked by a procession of people, until one day someone believed in them and gave them a chance to excel.

Ezekiel describes how a tender shoot is planted on a high mountain, and grows into a majestic tree. Jesus in Mark's gospel relates the parable of the growth of the mustard seed. The farmer goes about the task of sowing and cultivating seed. 'Without his knowing how it happens,' the seed grows, steadily and surely, until it has become a great crop, ripe for the harvest.

The key to understanding this parable from Mark's gospel, and Ezekiel's imagery, is to realise that God is responsible for the growth of both tree and seed. The kingdom of God will grow and develop 'without our knowing how it happens,' and in spite of all our faults and foibles, because it belongs to, originates in and is ever attended by God.

Yet we have a role to play in the growth of others. We can be the nourishment for others' growth. In Mark's gospel, Jesus gives us this small parable to illustrate the kingdom of God and he suggests that kingdom lies within us. The parable of the mustard seed and tree planted on the mountain top contrast small beginnings with powerful results. It contrasts the hidden with the manifest: the seed is hidden in the earth and only becomes visible in the plant.

1. Patricia Datchuck Sanchez, *Celebration: An Ecumenical Worship Resource*, (Kansas City, Missouri: National Catholic Reporter Company, Inc., May, 2003).

So too it is with the kingdom of God proclaimed by Jesus. We all have the potential within us to blossom into solid Christians. We all have the hidden gift of Christ within us.

Today we come here to celebrate the life of Christ and his gift to us and we publicly acknowledge and celebrate our willingness to commit to a journey of faith-filled life. We promise to be present to each other and to support each other. We aspire to achieve our highest goals in our Christian lives, reaching own fullest potential. Just like the mustard seed needs water to blossom forth, we too need an added condition: we need to believe that Christ lies within each one of us – we need faith.

We ought to believe in one another. We are called to nourish the gift of faith within ourselves, and, most especially, in young people such as our children.

In much the same way that Thomas Edison's mother believed in his natural talents and encouraged him in developing those talents, we also need to be encouraged in our faith. We need to stretch out to one another and support others in their faith and invite them to develop a personal relationship with God through private prayer.

We hope to blossom together into mature Christians. We see Christ within others and hope others see Christ within us. Together we hope to realise our fullest potential as Christians, and bring forth the kingdom of God.

I Believe in God Even Though I Cannot See

Why are you terrified? Do you not yet have faith?
It was 3 am, May 10th, 1989 in Ireland and my sister was bang-
ing on my bedroom door trying to awaken me. We had just received a phone call from my best friend's parents, giving me
what was the worst news of my life up to that point – that my
best friend, Jim, had died in a plane crash while on a pilot training course in Vero Beach, Florida. I was devastated, absolutely
devastated!

Jim and I had become inseparable friends and I had been
looking forward to his return from the United States. The pain
pierced my heart and I mourned for months over his death. He
was only 24 and we had still much of life to share together. I will
never forget that pain that made my heart bleed.

As I mourned tearfully with Jim's family, I joined them in
questioning the existence of God. How could God let such a ter-
rible thing happen to such a good person like Jim? How could
God let this happen to me? I was furious at God. Actually, I was
so angry with God that after the funeral I would not return to a
church for over six months. Yet I realised I was worse without
God than with him.

Have you ever lost your faith in God? And how did God call
you back? Have you ever been so angry with God that you denied
his existence? Maybe you have lost a relative to death or lost a
long term serious relationship. Whatever it is, I'm sure we have
all doubted the existence of God at some stage or at least felt that
he was absent at some time in our lives. It is sometimes so hard
to believe while we are in the midst of wrenching pain, when we
have lost direct sight of God. We want to believe, but instead we
doubt.

As I look back to 1989, I see that my anger with God prevented
me from seeing his role in my life. Like a large item in front of
me, I could not see around my anger. I was blinded by my anger
and by my loss. I was blind to the many joys still in my life. I was
blind to the many other people who still loved me. I was blind to
the many cherished memories I had shared with Jim. I could not
see God in my life, and I was in the darkness.

In the same way, when we look up in the sky during the day,

we see the sun and acknowledge its existence. But then at night we cannot see it anymore. Sometime, we can see the sun's reflection through the moon. And then there are nights we don't even have the moon and we are in complete darkness. Where do we think the sun and the moon have gone? Have they disappeared? No. They are still present – we just can't see them directly. But we still believe in the sun, even when we cannot see it.

And so it is with God. There are times we can see him directly in our lives. In those moments, we are due no more credit for believing in him than the person who believes in the sun when it shines on their face. But there are other times in our lives when we cannot see God directly and we must rely on his reflection through others. And still there are other times when we can't see him at all. In those moments, like the disciples, we may doubt.

In these difficult moments of our lives Jesus knows that we, like his disciples, are not wicked unbelievers, but people who are tempted to panic in moments of crisis. The disciples forgot that God is ever-present and there was no need to panic. We, too, often forget that God is always there for us, even though we cannot see his presence. We have no need to panic because he will never forsake us.

We live in a demanding world and there are many opportunities to lose faith. The anxieties mount and we can end up travelling some tragic and lonely roads. But without faith we lose Jesus, our guide and companion. And when the storms of doubt arise, we cry out to him as did the disciples. He, who is the Lord of the storm, will be our navigator and will still both the wind and the sea. He will lead us to our desired haven. We need to believe, even though we cannot see him. We need to choose to believe, so we can say:

'I believe in the sun – even when it does not shine;
I believe in love – even when it is not shown;
I believe in God – even when he does not speak.'[1]

---

1. These words were written by a victim of the World War II Holocaust under a Star of David.

Merrily Move Towards Christ

There is a story told of a tired traveller who came to the banks of a river. Unfortunately there was no bridge by which he could cross. It was winter, and the surface of the river was covered with ice. It was getting dark, and the traveller wanted to reach the other side while there was enough light to see. He debated about whether or not the ice would bear his weight. Finally, after much hesitation and fear, he got down on his hands and knees and began, very cautiously, to creep across the surface of the ice. He hoped that by distributing his weight through his hands and knees, the ice would be less apt to break under the load. After he made his slow and painful journey about halfway across the river, he suddenly heard the sound of singing behind him. Out of the dusk, there came a four-horse load of coal, driven by a man singing merrily as he went his carefree way.

Here was the traveller, fearfully inching his way on his hands and knees. And there, as if whisked along by the winter's wind, went the driver, his horses, his sled, and the heavy load of coal over the same river![1]

This story illustrates how so many of us go through life. Some of us stand on the banks of the river, frozen with indecision, unable to make up our minds about the course to take. Others stand on the banks trying to muster enough courage to cross over to the other side of the task or problem encountered. Still others, like the traveller, crawl and creep through life for fear of thin ice. Often our faith is not strong enough to hold us up. Still, there are those who whisk along, whistling happily as they go. Their faith is unshakable because it is faith in God.

In today's gospel we hear about two people who have unshakable faith: the synagogue official named Jairus and the woman afflicted with hemorrhages for twelve years. They move with purpose toward Jesus. Jairus pleads with Jesus to come to his house and lay his hands on his little girl. He believed that Jesus could heal his sick little girl if only he laid his hands on her. And Jairus was right, for she was healed in his sight.

---

1. Brian Cavanaugh, *The Sower's Seeds*, (Mahwah, New Jersey: Paulist Press, 1990).

The woman with hemorrhages had enough faith in Jesus that she believed if she could only touch the tassel of his garment, then she would be immediately healed of her ailment. And she was right. She was healed immediately.

They both believed in Jesus. They both moved with purpose towards Jesus and both received their reward of healing.

We, too, are called to be disciples of Jesus today. We are called to move toward him with great purpose. We are called to believe in him, for he will bring us healing. Sometimes we experience physical illness and we want healing. Other times we experience emotional distress and we want healing.

In these times, we often move through life, inching along, waiting for something to come to us. Instead, we ought to go at life knowing that God will give us healing. Sometimes that healing will be physical and, through the care of doctors, nurses and medicine, our ailment abates. But most often the healing that God gives us is that of acceptance of the reality of our human lives, and the natural limitations of our human bodies.

God will give us the strength to endure the suffering and the peace to accept the final time if it comes soon. When we have faith in God and his ever-dwelling Spirit within us, we do not have to fear, nor do we have to creep through life as if moving on thin ice over a frozen river.

Instead, we are called to have unshakeable faith in Jesus and move toward him with great purpose. Today and this week, with God's help we can merrily make our way through life.

Admit Your Weakness
and Be Strong in Christ

I remember many years ago when I went on my first youth retreat as a leader. I was a small group leader, in charge of ten young boys and girls. My main role was to facilitate discussion about various topics among the ten youth assigned to my group for the weekend. I remember my friend and I driving up to the isolated camp on a Friday night. On the trip in the car, he coached me on what to do and what not to do.

Having given presentations to large groups of business people on and off for years, I must admit I was not really listening much. Then came my first group session and I was terrified. I had never talked about my faith in any group setting and trying to get the young boys and girls to talk was impossible.

After the first discussion my friend asked me how things were going. I told him it was dreadful and I would prefer to crawl under a rock. I really wanted to go home right there and then. I've never felt like such a failure as I did that night. My friend suggested that I relay that sense of failure to the students. I struggled with doing so, assuming they would laugh at me.

And the second session went as bad as the first. This time I went to my friend and insisted that I get the keys to the car because I was driving home that night! He did not oblige and again reiterated the best approach was to come clean with the group and tell them this was my first time. 'They will understand your weakness,' he assured me.

After our little conversation I prayed about it in the corner of the room, pleading with God to deliver me from these little terrors! But God assured me in much the same way my friend had. So off I went to the small group of youth, who I visualised waiting like wolves, licking their lips for their next meal. Terrified and shaking with anxiety, I announced to the youth how fearful I was and how I felt like a complete failure that night. I wanted to be some help but I felt inadequate for their needs.

One could taste the sense of relief dissipate. To my shock and amazement each of the students, slowly opened up, sharing how they all felt the same way. The rest of the evening and weekend was an amazing experience of faith sharing and bonding. Yet I had to face my weakness and allow God to minister through it.

In today's second reading to the church at Corinth, Paul struggles with some 'thorn in his flesh' that he pleaded with God to take away three times. But God's only answer is that 'his grace is sufficient.' God tells Paul, and us, that in times of struggle he will give us strength and courage, and that all we have to do is come to him. The power of Christ will come through our weakness and make us strong. If we allow Christ to dwell within us then he will make us strong in our times of struggle.

Of course, this is easy to say but not so easy to do. When faced with our inadequacies or failures, we often find excuses for ourselves or quickly project blame onto others. We find any reason but our own actions for the current crisis.

It is hard to accept the reality of our weakness or failure. It is hard to accept that we cannot measure up to our expectations. It is hard to not be all we had hoped to be. But God says that he will make us strong through our weakness, if only we come to him through Christ. If we can come to rely on him in all things, then he will make us strong in our weakness. Even if it is our own family and friends who reject us, he will be there to keep and hold us. He will always be there to make us strong.

But to be strong in Christ we need to be one in Christ. This requires us to be attentive to him and to be ready to admit, sometimes publicly, our weakness, because only then he is free to reign in our lives.

This week, God will make us strong if we are one in Christ.

Advocate For Others

Sister Dorothy Stang was a Sister of Notre Dame de Namur from Dayton, Ohio. The 74-year-old nun had spent 35 years in Brazil, the last 22 living and working among 400 poor farmers and their families in Anapu, Para, a section of Brazil's Amazon rain forest. A slight, unassuming woman of boundless energy and irrepressible joy, Sister Dorothy had become an effective advocate for not only the poor but for the rain forest itself, one of the world's most important environments, and one that is rapidly being destroyed by powerful economic interests.

But the nun's work with the landless and her efforts to preserve the rain forest were too troublesome for the wealthy logging and ranching interests. On February 12, 2005, Sister Dorothy was ambushed by two men, who had been hired by a local rancher. Witnesses said that Sister Dorothy, when confronted by the gunmen, took her Bible from her bag and began reading aloud. The two gunmen listened for a moment, then stepped back and fired. She died instantly from six gunshots wounds.

Sister Dorothy knew that her work was dangerous, but refused police protection for herself. 'I don't want to flee, nor do I want to abandon the battle of these farmers, who live without any protection of the forest. They have a sacrosanct right to aspire to a better life on land, where they can work with dignity while respecting the environment.'[1]

In our western world today we do not have many martyrs or prophets. Few of us are willing to stand up and give our lives for a particular ideal, no matter how strong our convictions about the cause. Few of us are dedicated enough to a mission that we will go out and spend our lives serving that mission. Few of us have convictions for which we are willing to die.

Yet in today's gospel, Jesus sends the disciples out two by two to proclaim the good news. They are to take nothing for their journey. They are told to go without food, sack, or money. They are told to go and be prepared to accept what is offered to them. They are told to go and preach repentance. And they did.

1. Connections, (Mediaworks, Londonderry, NH: April, 2005)

Clearly, they were not welcomed in some places and were driven from those places, wiping the dust off their shoes. Eventually their missions would end in a martyr's death. They were prophets and martyrs for their time, and many thousands of people got to hear the message of Christ because of their conviction to preach the gospel always.

In a similar manner, Amos in the first reading was a prophet of his time, even though he protests that title. For his part, Amos was commissioned by God to criticise and to energise the early community of Israel. A native of Judah and a migrant worker, Amos did not aspire to the prophetic ministry, nor did he refuse the call of God when he perceived it. Amos was not afraid to proclaim what God has asked of him. He spoke difficult words of challenge to Amaziah, the royal household priest who was no longer listening to God's word for the king. Amaziah banished Amos because he did not like what he was saying, but not before Amos got to proclaim the words of God. He was a prophet who was never afraid to proclaim God's word.

We are the disciples of Christ in today's world. We, too, are sent by Christ to proclaim the good news to all. We may not be sent two by two without food, clothes, or money, to eventually end in a martyr's death. We may not be commissioned by God to take on the local government. But we are sent to be ready to confront the injustices we encounter. We are called to speak out for those who are oppressed, whether in our local communities or in foreign lands. We are called to give voice to the voiceless of the immigrants among us. We are called to open our eyes to the needs of those who are jobless, homeless or friendless.

Today, we may not be called to give our life in martyrdom, but we are called to be a disciple, and an advocate for others in need.

Great Pyrenee of the Flock

Last week I was watching the Discovery Channel and I saw an interesting programme about the lost art of shepherding. It was a fascinating programme about how shepherds do their work and how their sheepdogs are an essential component of their work. The shepherd typically has two dogs to assist him in his role – the Border Collie and the Great Pyrenee. The Border Collie is, as the name suggests, the one who sets the borders for the sheep. He is the world's premiere sheepdog, unsurpassed in terms of patience, agility and stamina. The Border Collie goes ahead of the sheep to make sure they take the right path and then returns to ensure they remain on the path, running back and forth to keep the sheep in the fold.

On the other hand, the Great Pyrenee is the companion dog with the sheep. He is white-furred and large, like sheep, and looks like a sheep from the distance. He thinks he is a sheep and sheep think he is one of them. He stays with the sheep all day, protecting them from within their ranks. When a predator comes close, his ferocious bark is heard all over the valley or mountain where the sheep are grazing. He guards the sheep from within their ranks and leads them by protecting them.

The shepherd has an important role in taking care of the sheep by taking care of the dogs. For example, it is important that the Great Pyrenee receives a very large meal before the day begins so that the huge 100 lb dog is well fed for the entire day. If not, out of hunger the dog will be distracted during the day and search for food through the rodents of the fields and not do his primary job of caring for the sheep. At the end of a long day the Great Pyrenee knows to come home when he feels hungry. He knows it is time to take the flock home, and when he arrives there is another large meal waiting for him. The Great Pyrenee will perform his job of protecting the sheep as long as he is well-fed, nourished and loved. This is the key to the success of the shepherd and his dogs' work.

In today's first reading from the Prophet Jeremiah, we hear how the Lord God warns against those who mislead and scatter flock of the pasture. The people, who had been misled and scattered, driven away and uncared for, and who lived in fear and trembling, placed their hopes for the future on a promised king. But centuries would pass before 'the Lord our justice' would appear in the person of Jesus, to seek out the strays and the lost and to gather all the people of God with love and righteousness.[1]

And in the gospel today we hear Jesus give more instructions to his disciples. This time he invites them to 'Come by yourselves to an out-of-way place and rest a little.' He had first told them to be apostles and to carry the message of salvation to others. They were sent into the field to work and protect the lost sheep. As Jesus had pastored and fed them, so they, in turn, would be commissioned to pastor the growing community of believers. Mark tells us that 'the apostles returned to Jesus and reported all that they had done and what they taught.' They now came back for nourishment, care and love.

Jesus frequently withdrew from the crowds and the demands of the ministry to 'rest' for a while to pray and be renewed. He encourages us to do the same. Like the shepherd's dog we, too, are sent into the field to care and protect each other in the pasture of our lives.

We are given nourishment here at this table each week, through the celebration of the Eucharist and we know that we are to return here for another meal after our work of the week is done. We come here to 'rest' today a while and be replenished.

May we know that next week a new meal awaits us.

1. Patricia Datchuck Sanchez, *Celebration: An Ecumenical Worship Resource*, (Kansas City, Missouri: National Catholic Reporter Company, Inc., Archives Online).

Basic Instinct

As many of you know, I just returned from a hiking trip to Yellowstone and Grand Teton National Parks, home to thousands of black bears and grizzly bears. One afternoon, a friend and I hiked in Grand Teton, climbing 3,000 feet to a place called Surprise Lake, located about 10,000 feet above sea level. As we hiked along the trail we admired the beauty of the manifold huckleberry bushes. As we gazed upon the magnificence of the surroundings, we came to our senses and realised that because it was early evening it was the ideal time for bears to feed themselves, and bears love to eat huckleberries. Then we noticed how many of the trees were marked with bear claws and how the trail was alongside a river teeming with fish. All of these things make for a dangerous place to be hiking in the early evening.

Fortunately, we did not encounter any bears, though it would have been fun to see them – from a distance! It is interesting to note how bears know exactly where to go to get their food. There are no signs telling the bears where to eat! They know by basic instinct. I think the same is true for us.

I think we know exactly where to go to get our food – the refrigerator or the store, right? Well, I am not talking about that sort of food. I am referring to spiritual food.

Most of us are aware of this internal yearning for the Lord. If we listen to our own basic instinct I believe that we know we can always go directly to the Lord for nourishment. I am not sure, however, that we always listen to our instinct; instead, we end up looking for this nourishment in other areas of our lives, such as our jobs, where we work endless hours seeking power or money. We seek satisfaction in our sports, where we spend endless hours physically working our bodies, or in our relationships where we use much emotional energy. None of these things are bad, in and of themselves – in fact, some are good – but they are not where we receive our spiritual nourishment.

In the scripture today, we hear from the sixth chapter of John's gospel and we begin the Bread of Life Discourse, outlining some theological and spiritual reflections on the meaning of the Eucharist for the Christian community. We will be reading from this gospel for the next several weeks and today begins with the fourth of seven signs of John's gospel, giving us the key to understanding this section.

In the first three gospels of the New Testament, (called the synoptic gospels because all three are very similar,) Jesus gives a blessing and then he gives his disciples the bread and fish to distribute to the crowds. However, in John's gospel Jesus feeds the people directly. Here lies the key to the reading – Jesus is the direct source of the nourishment.

We, as Catholics, know this by basic instinct because we celebrate the sacrament of the Eucharist weekly. While this is our primary source for nourishment, Jesus also told us that wherever two or three gather in his name he is there among them. So Jesus is our direct source of nourishment in a number of ways: through the sacraments, through personal prayer, and through communal prayer.

The challenge for us then is to allow ourselves the space to develop our basic instinct. We need to attune our native listening skills. If we do so, we will instinctively know where to go for nourishment. To do this, I believe, we need to allow ourselves some time in personal prayer so that the Lord can feed us. Then we can come to this table for even more nourishment. Of course, we know this by basic instinct and that is why we are here in church.

Maybe there are other people in our lives who we know are spiritually starving and who no longer listen to their basic instinct. Maybe we can invite them to this table so that the Lord can nourish them again. Just like going to a social function, it is always easier to go with someone than to go alone. So it is with coming to church; if we have someone to go with then it becomes a little easier.

This week may we remember that the Lord answers all our needs and offers us constant nourishment for our spiritual selves. May we bring ourselves, and invite others, to this table for nourishment and so listen to our basic instinct.

Eighteenth Sunday in Ordinary Time
Exod 16:2-2, 12-15; Ps 78; Eph 4:17, 20-24; Jn 6:24-35

Getting What We Need

About once a month I go to the mega store, Costco, to get groceries for the rectory. When shopping there I have a bad habit of walking from aisle to aisle. Then I see something that I simply 'must have' and 'I cannot do without it'. So I end up buying maybe a twelve pack or larger of that item!

However, I have a friend who shops at Costco more regularly than I. When he goes into the store he goes directly to the items that he needs to purchase. He takes less than a half hour to do his shopping, while I always take over an hour! He ends up buying only what he needs and I end up buying more than I need.

Does that ever happen to you? You go into the store to buy certain items and you end up buying all these extra items.

In today's first reading the Lord tells Moses that he will rain down food from heaven and each day the people are to gather their daily portion. And so the people of Israel have their fill with bread each morning and quail each evening. There are two important points here: that the Lord supplies our need for food and that we are to take only what we need! In other words, we are to put our trust in the Lord and seek only what is essential.

This message is enhanced in the gospel when Jesus tells us that he is the bread come down from heaven. If we come to him then he will satisfy our every hunger and every thirst. Jesus challenges us to seek only what is truly essential. However, as we move through the mega store of our own lives and go about living each and every day, most of us focus on our *desires*, and not necessarily on our *needs*. In other words, hoping to satisfy the internal emptiness, we seek to fill our lives with material things from this world.

Not that we deliberately turn away from God, but by choosing to spend our time and effort on other things we leave no time or energy for our primary source of spiritual food in God. We often overwork, leaving no time for our treasured human relationships, relationships with our spouses, children and friends. Frequently we race from one place to the next place, with such a hurried pace that there is no room for casual conversation that could enliven our days. We try to achieve so much with our to-do lists each day, while prayer is often not even on the list of priorities.

The challenge from the scriptures today is to refocus our priorities according to our needs and not just our desires. Yes, it would be nice to have a bigger house or nicer car, but if it means working longer hours, then those things are hardly essential to our lives. Yes, it would be nice to get that promotion or raise, but if it means sacrificing our time with family it is hardly essential to our lives. Yes, it would be nice to play or watch more sports, but if it means I have less time for important relationships then it is hardly essential to my life. Yes, it would nice to make more time available to others, but if it means that I have no time for God then it is hardly essential.

Today, we are called to make Jesus, the bread of life, a priority in our daily lives. Yes, we come here on Sundays and that is awesome – but we are challenged this week to make Jesus a priority every day.

May we not become Costco shoppers of life, taking what we do not need just because it is there and we think we might want it; instead, may we take what we truly need: time with the Lord each day.

Today, let us come to the Lord, who is the Bread of Life.

Bread for Others

Recently I saw the movie *Hurricane*. It is the true story of a black boxer in the 1960s, Ruben Hurricane Carter, who was framed for a murder and falsely convicted. It is a compelling story of how racism and hatred can have profound consequences.

In his hasty and unconstitutional trial, Hurricane was found guilty and sentenced to spend the rest of his natural life in prison. He protested his innocence but to no avail.

There are several powerful and pivotal scenes in the movie, but for me the turning point was when, after several denied appeals to have his case retried, Hurricane gets word back that his latest appeal, some 19 years after his conviction, has been denied again. He then calls one of his friends who has always believed in his innocence and says he simply cannot do the time any more. He cannot continue!

It is a heart-breaking scene because we realise that this powerful man's spirit has been broken. He implies that he will kill himself or get the guards to kill him. Finishing his life in jail was no longer possible. He could not live in prison any longer.

In a desperate effort to give him hope, his friends moved from Toronto, Canada into a building facing the prison and stayed there until he won his freedom. They gave him the hope he needed to live.

Hurricane spent 20 years in jail for a crime he did not commit, but eventually won his freedom in 1983.

In the first reading today from the book of Kings, we hear of Elijah, in the depths of despair. He collapses under a broom tree and prays for death. Elijah had done all the Lord asked of him and had spoken eloquently against the false prophets of his Queen Jezebel, but then he was banished and had to flee for his life. We find him today worn out and discouraged, he is 'a day's journey into the desert ' without water or food. He was faithful to God, yet we find him praying for death. It is in this moment of rock bottom that Elijah realises he is completely dependent on God for life itself. He is desperate and turns directly to God in appeal. God hears his call and feeds him with food and drink brought by the angels .

Elijah had become desperate and was completely dependent on God.

At this point I would like to try an experiment, but I need your help and your cooperation. I want everyone to hold your breath for a while. Don't start yet! Let me explain first. Before you hold your breath, listen for my instructions. As you hold your breath, I want you to become aware of your need for air. Listen to your body and become aware of that desperate need. As you hold it longer and longer, feel the need for air. Hold it as long as you can without passing out. I do not want to call 911 emergency for anyone!

Okay; if everyone is ready, then *hold your breath!*

When you were holding your breath, could you feel the need for air? Every minute of every day we breathe, and yet, we are hardly aware of it. Ordinarily, we are not aware our need for air because we can breathe. However, when we cannot breathe we become aware very quickly of our absolute dependence on air. We cannot survive for much more than a minute or two. But rarely are we conscious of this need.

The same can be said of spiritual food from God. Only when we do not have it do we suddenly become aware of our desperate need for it. Are we aware of our spiritual need for God in our lives? If we stop and hold our spiritual breath for a minute we will realise that our spiritual lungs heave for God, for spiritual food. That is one of the reasons we come here to this table – to be fed some bread of life and to help us get through the week.

But there is more to this spiritual hunger than one hour of communal worship can fill. We are called to be bread for others. We are called to take from this table a morsel of love and pass it to others through the week. We are invited to take note of our spiritual hunger and others' hunger too. We are called to be bread for one another.

Now, let's do the exercise again, except this time let us focus on our need for God in our lives, as our lungs heave for air. Is there someone in our lives for whom we can be bread this week? Jesus tells us that he is the living bread, come down from heaven, and anyone who eats this bread shall live forever. Like Hurricane's friends who gave him hope in the midst of despair, we are called to give others hope in the midst of their broken lives. Christ Jesus is the bread of life.

This week we can be the bread of life for others.

Food and Guide for the Journey

My brother and his wife are away on vacation and are preparing to climb Mt Kilimanjaro in northern Tanzania, on the border with Kenya in Africa. They have been getting in shaping for some time now and are ready to take on Kibo summit. When they arrive at the mountain they will be required to take a guide with them for the journey. This guide will show them the exact route to take and guide them up the sometimes treacherous climb.[1] At the end of the climb, they will reach the summit, at 19,331 feet and covered in snow, and will have one of the finest views in the world, with Tanzania on one side and Kenya on the other. However, it is considered unwise to attempt the climb without an experienced guide for the journey. Indeed, they are not even allowed to do so.

I thought to myself, how interesting! We go through our journey of life and it is difficult and treacherous at times. It seems we could do with a guide for the journey.

In today's second reading from the letter to the Ephesians, we are warned to act like wise people and use current opportunities to make the best of life. It informs us that some actions are unwise and we should listen to the will of the Father, listen to the wisdom of God.

In the first reading from the Book of Proverbs, wisdom, personified as a woman, puts on a banquet and we are invited to feast on wisdom's food.

In the gospel, Jesus tells us that he is that wisdom-food. He is the bread come down from heaven. We have been reading from the sixth chapter of John's gospel and this section has two traditions of understanding. On the one hand some maintain that 'the bread of life' refers to Jesus' flesh, and so we have the 'Eucharistic' understanding, as celebrated at every Mass. On the other hand, we have those who maintain that these passages are strictly metaphor, pointing to 'food as wisdom,' in line with the first reading.

Which tradition is accurate? The answer is: they both are!

---

1. Inspired by a story given in *Homily Helps*, (St Anthony Messenger Press: Cincinnati, OH, August, 2003)

John's gospel is riddled with double meanings, and this passage is no exception. Jesus Christ is both the wisdom and real food. Jesus Christ is both the guide and the food for the journey.

Yes, God offers wisdom to all who seek. However, unlike my brother and his wife going up the Kilimanjaro Mountain, we have a choice. We can accept or ignore Christ, accept or ignore him as our wise guide for the journey; we can try the journey on our own. I suspect that most of us have attempted at least a section on our own. Dare I say it, I remember as a young man I thought I knew how to climb the summit of life and I set off on my own without God or Christ. Soon I discovered that this mountain was too much for me. I got lost and called out for help.

No matter how far we get up the mountain, or how lost we get on this journey of life, God always offers us his guide, his Son to help us back. God always offers Christ as both our guide and food for the journey of life. When we come here each Sunday we eat his food and we are spiritually nourished for another leg of the journey.

But if we are serious about Christ being our guide we need to set aside some time to listen to his wisdom. We have all become very busy people, with very little free time to do anything. I know that many of you are retired but many of you tell me how, now that you are retired, you are surprised how little time you seem to have. You wonder how you found time to work! Yes, we have become very busy people young or old, working or retired, at school or at home.

I believe we need to slow down to listen to wisdom. We need to find some time each day to spend with the Lord, so that the Wise Counsellor can give us his wisdom. We need to open our minds and hearts to the will of the Father, and that requires listening time. This week maybe we can carve some time out of each day and listen to the Lord's advice for our journey. Jesus Christ, who is the 'bread of Life', is both guide and food for the journey.

Drilling Deeper for Faith

Oil companies drill for oil when they know that it is relatively close to the earth's surface. The deeper the oil, the more expensive it is to locate and bring to the surface. The easier it is to bring to the surface, the quicker and bigger the return is on a company's investment. The less they spend on bringing the oil up, the more profit they will have to keep.[1] This strategy makes perfect economic sense.

However, if it is applied to faith in God, the strategy falls apart. The faith of an adult cannot be based solely on 'easy or immediate' rewards. Life is not that simple. Instead a person's faith must be based on commitment – the commitment to go deeper with our faith, continually and constantly; the commitment to drill deep into our own hearts where God alone is; the commitment to drill deep into our own minds to understand God's will for us.

Each day can bring new challenges to yesterday's faith. Yesterday we believed in God and his plan for us but today we doubt his presence. Most of us can remember saying or thinking something like: it was easier to believe in God before my girlfriend broke up with me; or it was easier to believe in God before I lost my job; or it was easier to believe in God before my brother/sister/mother died; or it was easier to believe in God before I was diagnosed with cancer.

I know many of you have come to me with questions of doubt such as, 'Where is God now, with the war in Iraq?' or 'Where is God in the middle of all the Middle East violence?' or, more personally, 'Where was God when my father was dying?'

In challenges of daily life we often find ourselves doubting God's existence in our lives. So where do we go?

In today's gospel we hear that many of Jesus' disciples began to doubt him after hearing his Bread of Life Discourse. These same disciples had seen his miracles and heard him speak. They had been amazed by his brilliance, calling him Son of God, a great prophet and Wonder Worker. He must be the Messiah

---

1. *Homily Helps*, (St Anthony Messenger Press: Cincinnati, OH, August, 2003)

they had exclaimed! They had seen with their own eyes and heard with their own ears.

But now Jesus' words were challenging them too much. He was asking them to eat of his flesh and drink of his blood. It was just too much! They reconsidered everything again. They thought that maybe what they saw was not real or that what they heard was not so brilliant. Yes, as soon as the first challenge came, they were gone. Their faith was so shallow that it could not last. They did not drill any deeper than the surface.

However, Peter answered as a person of deeper faith. He speaks for the twelve who remained with Jesus despite his challenging words. Peter was in for the long haul as he proclaimed, 'You have the words of eternal life. We have come to believe and are convinced that you are the God's Holy One.' Peter had drilled deeper into his heart, responding to God's gift of faith, as he remained open to the Spirit.

We too are invited to drill deeper into own hearts to be prepared for the challenges of tomorrow. We are all here today and we believe in the presence of Christ in the bread and wine. However, we need to continually drill deeper to be ready for the challenges of life. Today is the day to drill deeper.

Coming here is a start, but we know it is not enough. We need to find time to pray and be with the Lord each day. It is only with quiet time alone in prayer that we can be nourished in wisdom. How can he feed us if we are too busy to eat his food?

Yes, we need to take some time each day to drill more deeply, to drill into the depths of our own hearts where God alone is waiting with rich resources. Today let us make the commitment to drill deeper, and respond to God's gift of faith and be open to the Spirit!

Dignity as a Child of God

A friend of mine who works as a teacher also works on weekends as a housekeeper to support his family, particularly his sick mother. One day, as he was cleaning the house of the couple he works for, some of the couple's friends came to visit. From the moment they arrived until the moment they left, they pointed out rather bluntly how the room was still dirty and he should clean the furniture again. They looked down on him and his menial cleaning job. At one point they even laughed at his clothes. They treated him like a third class citizen. Although the couple was embarrassed by their guests' behaviour, they said and did nothing. As you can imagine, my friend was deeply hurt by the incident, since he had done nothing wrong to them.

That following week school started for him and he returned to a new class of boys and girls. My friend is truly an excellent teacher and after only a few weeks the children loved him dearly, lauding him to their parents with unusual fondness. A few weeks went by and a parents' conference came up. As parents arrived they were eager to meet their children's new teacher whom all seemed to love so much. To my friend's shock, the couple that had treated him so badly were the parents of the one of his new students.

As their eyes met there were a few moments of embarrassment. The parents were shocked that their child's wonderful teacher was the housekeeper they had abused the previous week. They were faced with the reality of their own actions and how inconsistent it was with their professed Catholic faith. My friend never said a word and, unfortunately, neither did the couple. They lacked the courage to face the reality of their own hypocrisy.

Sometimes I think we divide the world into three groups. We have the inner circle where our friends and want-to-be friends are; these we treat with great respect and attention. Then we have the next circle, full of our acquaintances and co-workers; these we give some time to but no real quality attention. Then we have the outer circle where those we know very little or do not really wish to know remain; these we often treat as if they are invisible, giving them little or no attention. At first we might say to ourselves, 'That is not true! I do not treat people like that!'But how many of us know the names of the janitors in our offices or even greet them with a kind smile or conversation? What about the people who work in our gardens or who bus our tables at restaurants? So often I have been witness to such people being treated with disdain.

The world is full of people who work with their hands in our gardens and fields, and who work with their hands on our floors and roofs, and who work with their hands in our toilets. They all deserve our respect.

In the second reading today we listen to the letter of James. This letter makes it abundantly clear that we are to be more than just hearers of the word: we are also to be doers of the word. He says that we ought not to delude ourselves. We need to do more than come here and pray at church; we need to be doers of the word in the world we live. The example he gives is to take care of the poor and oppressed, as represented by widows and orphans.

Elsewhere in scripture it tells us that we are all children of God. There really is no difference between those workers and us; we are all children of God. Every last one of us was made in God's image, and every last one of us is entitled to be treated with dignity. Whether we work in a fancy office as an engineer, secretary, or executive, or whether we work with our hands in the fields, on the floors, or in toilets, we are all entitled to be treated with respect.

Tomorrow we as a nation celebrate Labour Day and we acknowledge the work of all people, especially those we rarely see or credit for their hard work. Like the couple my friend cleans house for, sometimes we witness abuse or mistreatment of workers. May hearing the gospel today give us the courage to speak out when necessary to defend the dignity of all. To say to someone who is mistreating that busboy or waiter, 'Hey, stop that behaviour.' To say to someone who is mistreating that grocery clerk, 'Hey, stop that behaviour.' To say to ourselves, 'Hey stop that behaviour.'

This week may we treat all people with respect, from the janitor to the gardener, from the field worker to the housekeeper, from the teacher to the office clerk. May we be willing to treat all people with dignity, as children of God.

Be Open

A young couple and their two children returned from vacation in the Great Smoky Mountains National Park with happy memories and tons of photos. However, they also came back a little shaken. On the third day into their vacation, their son, who was deaf from birth, wandered away from the campsite. His parents went searching for him frantically, calling for him in vain. Eventually, they caught up with him meandering down a service road, his back to an oncoming delivery truck. Although the driver was honking his horn and his parents were shouting frantically, the boy heard nothing. Fortunately tragedy was adverted when the truck screeched to a halt just short of the boy. The parents realised with great clarity the dangers their boy faced through his challenge of being deaf.[1]

Sometimes we walk through life spiritually deaf. We often meander down the road of life doing what we want to do, completely deaf to the words of God. We have a spiritual tragedy barrelling down behind us and we know nothing about it. I know that there was a time in my life when I was sure about the way I wanted to lead my life and that way did not include God. A spiritual disaster was barrelling down behind me and I rarely knew it. But even now that I am a priest, I often find myself so busy that I sometimes do not hear what God is trying to tell me. I suspect that we all fall into that trap of busy lives. I suspect that we sometimes are deaf to God.

We hear in today's reading how Jesus heals the man born deaf. He is released from his bondage and set free from ailment. But the word Jesus uses is important. He says, 'Ephphatha' which means, 'Be opened.' This has more to do with a disposition than it does a physical state. In other words, it is as much a spiritual healing as it is a physical healing. Immediately, the man is healed. I wonder if we can hear these words today and 'be opened' to the word of God in our lives. I know we come

---

1. Patricia Datchuck Sanchez, *Celebration: An Ecumenical Worship Resource*, (Kansas City, Montana: National Catholic Reporter Company, Inc., September, 2003).

here on Sundays and we try, but how else can we open ourselves to hear God's words?

God speaks to us in different ways. We need to be open to
these different ways if we are to really hear what he is saying.
First, God speaks to us through our family and friends, as well as
through those with whom we work or go to school. It might be
some words of challenge that they give us, or in the way they
criticise some of our actions. Maybe it is words of affirmation,
something positive they say to us.

Second, God speaks to us through nature and the wonder of
creation. Whether we hear the sound of a bird chirping from a
branch or whether we hear the sound of traffic, the gift of hearing is something to be thankful for. Indeed, our health is something to thankful for. Yes, the beauty of God's creation is always
screaming at us.

Third, God speaks to us through scripture, the written word
of God. Yes, we hear the Word of God proclaimed here on
Sundays, for as long as seven or maybe ten minutes at most. Is
that really enough to listen to what God is saying? Maybe we
can read the Bible on other days of the week.

Finally, God speaks to us within ourselves. He dwells within
the sanctuary of our hearts, where he alone guides us. It is this
last thing, God dwelling within us, upon which all the rest depends. I mean, if we do not believe God dwells within us then
we will not believe that God dwells within anyone else, and we
will find it hard to see God in creation or scripture.

So this week, can we cut out some time and space to listen to
what God is telling us directly? Maybe then we can actually hear
what God is saying to us through our family, friends or co-
workers. Maybe then we can hear what God is saying through
the beauty of creation or the gift of health. Maybe then we can
hear what God is saying through the scripture we hear each day.

'Ephphatha – Be Open.'

Who Do People Say That We Are?

When I was a young child, family friends would say how I looked like father or my mother. 'Oh, you have your mother's nose.' 'Look at little Brendan, doesn't he have his father's eyes!' When I got a little older other friends would say how I looked like my older brothers. I looked more like Gerard than Kevin, or more like Martin than Danny. As many of you know I am the youngest of twelve, so there was always plenty of comparison between my brothers and I. But even now people tell me how alike our family looks. At a recent family gathering the constant refrain was, 'Oh Brendan, you are the spitting image of your mother!' Also, many people say how I can act like some of my close friends. My comments or mannerisms seem to be similar to those with whom I spend most of my time.

Do you ever get compared to your brothers or sisters or friends? Do you remember as a child being compared to your parents? Do people say even now how you look like someone in your family?

In the gospel today we hear about the identity of Jesus. Jesus asked his disciples, 'Who do people say that I am?' A flurry of answers is given, but then Jesus asks them who do they, the disciples, say that he is. Peter spoke for the disciples and announced, 'You are the Messiah, the Christ, the chosen one.' It was obvious to the disciples that he was the Messiah because they saw Jesus' actions and believed in him. And they were charged to spread that news, but not yet; Jesus must first die and then rise again.

Today, who do others say we are? I mean us here, at our parish community. Who do people say that we are? On Sunday we come here and praise and thank God for his role in our lives. But we do not live in this church, we live in the world. We live our lives outside of this church building and we are called to live our faith in action in our families, in our jobs, and in our communities. Do others know we are Catholics by our actions?

Let me make a suggestion. Why don't we become the most hospitable people we know. When we come to church here, people will know that they are welcome. We will smile at each other, even those we do not know. We will greet each other warmly, before and after Mass. We will talk to each other here, and outside when we see each other we will greet each other enthusiastically. We will become what we are, a community of believers. If we do this, then later in the Mass when we say the Lord's prayer together, holding hands will not be a sterile habit but a genuine connection with the person next to us and an authentic prayer as family. We will pray as a community of believers who ask for forgiveness as we forgive, who ask that his will be done in us as a community and as individuals.

I am new to this parish and have been here only a few months, but I already know you are a welcoming and warm community. Let us spread that community throughout our lives outside of this church.

Today we celebrate the Celebration Day for Catechists and in a few minutes we will commission those catechists in our community. They will commit to spreading the good news to all in our community. But we are all called to spread the good news to everyone in our lives, especially those outside the church.

Someone once described attending a Catholic church as standing on the banks of a flowing river, dying of thirst. Imagine that, standing on the banks of a flowing river, dying of thirst! Let no one stand on the banks of our river here at our parish and die of thirst. Let us be the water of life to all those around us. Let us be the water of life to all in our town.

Voice of a Child

In a short story by Leo Tolstoy, a Russian officer is captured by a group of peasants during the Russian revolution. Despised as an officer of the hated czar, the crowd demands the officer be killed. The officer, carrying himself with great dignity, resigns himself to his fate. As they lead him to the town square where he would be hung, the piercing sobs of a child are heard. 'Daddy, Daddy,' cries the six-year old as he pushes his way through the crowd to get closer to the prisoner. 'Daddy! What are they going to do to you? Wait, wait, take me with you, take me!' Someone in the crowd says: 'Go home boy – go to your mother.' But the condemned officer hears his son's voice. 'He has no mother!' the officer shouts. At last the boy reaches his father and grabs his father's arm. The crowd continues to demand, 'Kill him! Hang him!' The little boy is now terrified: 'What are they going to do you, Daddy?' 'Listen, I want you to do something for me,' the father says reassuringly. 'You know Catherine, our neighbour. Run to her house. Stay with her. I'll be there very soon.' But the boy refuses to leave his father. 'They're going to kill you, Daddy!' 'Oh no, this is just a game, they're just playing.' The father gently pushes his son away from him and then speaks quietly to one of the mob's leaders. 'Listen, kill me if you want and whenever you want, but not in the presence of my child. Untie my hands for two minutes and hold my hand. Show my child that you are my friend and you plan no harm and then he will leave us. Then … then you can tie me again and kill me any way you want.'

The leader of the crowd agrees and unties him. The prisoner takes his son into his arms. 'Be a good boy now, and go to Catherine's. I'll be home soon.' The boy stares at his father for what seems like an eternity. 'You'll really come home?' 'I will. I promise. Now go to Catherine's.' 'Will you?' 'I promise,' says the father. The boy seems relieved and obeys his father. A woman leads him from the crowd.

When the child disappears from sight, the officer draws his breath. 'I am ready. You may kill me now.' But something had happened to the crowd. The spirit of hatred and vengeance that had fueled the crowd's anger had gone. 'Let him go,' one

woman says. 'God will be his judge,' says another. Soon everyone takes up the chant. The prisoner's captors untie him.
Unbound, the proud officer breaks into tears. He puts his hands
over his face. And then he runs home through the crowd to keep
his promise to his little boy. The innocent love of a child for his
father transforms hatred and vengeance into love and forgiveness.[1]

Sometimes, we act like the crowd in this story, ready to judge
and condemn people from a distance. Maybe it is people in a
land distant from here, people we know very little about. Maybe
it is someone at the office with whom we disagree, and we have
joined the coffee room gossip about them. Maybe it is someone
else with whom we disagree philosophically, theologically, soc-
ially, or politically and we condemn them.

Yet not far from us is a child of a one kind or another who is
calling us to be forgiving and encouraging. Maybe we can act
like that child!

Christ in today's gospel challenges us to exchange our judge-
ments and ambitions for forgiveness and love. He tells us to welcome the child among us. Remember, the child in ancient Israel
was a symbol of powerlessness and oppression. So we are called
to welcome the inner voice that challenges us to move beyond
our judgments and to forgive.

Today, may we not go along with the crowd. Instead, may
we cry out for justice and forgiveness. Instead, may we be the
voice of the oppressed and powerless. Instead, may we be the
voice of the child.

---

1. Leo Tolstoy as quoted in *Connections*, (Mediaworks, Londonderry,
NH: September, 2003)

Twenty-sixth Sunday in Ordinary Time
Num 11:25-29; Ps 19; Jas 5:1-6; Mk 9:38-43, 45, 47-48

Open the Door to Christ

As many of you know, during the summer I was in Yellowstone National Park. Do you know that the mosquitoes are huge there? When they bite you they leave large scars. I mean, they whiz around the air like small birds and when they bite you it feels like a vampire is sucking blood from you. You even get lightheaded from the loss of blood. The bite leaves not just a mark that looks like a blister, but a mark the size of a music CD. Do you believe my description? No? Why not! Have you never seen a mosquito the size of a bird? Probably not. Okay, I was exaggerating a little. Okay, okay … maybe a lot! But what was my point in the short story? Yes, the mosquitoes are large and their bites hurt. This verbal style of language is called hyperbole. It is the use of exaggeration to make a point.

Well, in today's gospel, to make his very important point, Jesus uses this ancient rhetorical tool of hyperbole. He does not expect us to take what he says literally but he does intend us to take it seriously. While there are times when we need to take Jesus' words at face value, there are other times when we need to look more deeply into his words.

Today, we need to look below the surface. If we were to take these very harsh words literally, then I suspect that a lot of us would be missing some limbs, some of us might lose our eyes, and all of us would lose our tongues.

Who among us has never used our tongue to say something hurtful or wrong at some time? What Jesus is saying is that we have a choice. We have a choice to come and follow him and enjoy this life in fullness, as well as a reward in eternal life. If we choose to not follow him, then we will go to Gehenna. Remember Gehenna is actually a place outside Jerusalem.[1] It was considered condemned because some ancient kings had sacrificed their sons by burning them alive to appease the pagan gods. Israel considered it a place of sin and converted it into garbage dump where they burned their trash. So it was hot and smelly. This is how they imagined hell to be.

1. Patricia Datchuck Sanchez, *Celebration: An Ecumenical Worship Resource*, (Kansas City, Montana: National Catholic Reporter Company, Inc., September, 2003) 415.

So Jesus picks up on this thought and says if we do not do as he commanded us then we would spend eternity in Gehenna.The message from Jesus is very clear – we have a choice. We can choose to do good, or, to do evil. At this point I would like to show you a famous painting. *[Image of Light of the World comes onto large screens. It can also be seen at the following website: http://www.keble.ox.ac.uk/support/viewer.php?picture=75]*[2] from Keble College in England, and another rendition at St Paul's Cathedral in London. It was painted by William Holman Hunt in 1853 when he was just 21. However, he did not finish the painting until he was 29, and when he did he inscribed the back with, 'Forgive me Lord Jesus Christ, that I have kept you waiting so long.'

In this painting, the lantern is the light of conscience or truth, and the light around the head is the light of salvation. The door represents the human soul, which cannot be opened from the outside. There is no handle on the door, and the rusty nails and hinges overgrown with ivy denote that the door has never been opened and that the figure of Christ is asking for permission to enter. The writing under the picture is taken from Revelation 3: 'Behold I stand at the door and knock. If anyone can hear my voice and open the door I will come in and will be with them and they with me.'[3]

Like the gospel, this painting makes it very clear that it is our choice as to how we live. I know that in one sense I am preaching to the choir since you are all here at Sunday Mass. But some-times we turn away during the week. Sometimes we keep that door closed to Christ, maybe because we want to go to a party or somewhere and not be bothered by our conscience. Sometimes we keep that door closed to Christ because we want to go to our neighbours or co-workers and gossip about another neighbour/ friend while they are not there. Sometimes we keep that door closed to Christ because opening it disturbs our comfortable life style.

Yes, it is our choice and we know that sometimes we choose to keep it closed. It is only we who can open that door to Christ

---

2. Use of this image was inspired by William J. Bausch, *More Telling Stories Compelling Stories*, (Mystic, Connecticut: XXIIIrd Publications, 1993) p 1

3. As described on the website of Keble College, England (http:// www.keble.ox.ac.uk/life/chapel/light.php)

and invite his Holy Spirit into our hearts. And it is not a once-in-a-lifetime decision, but a daily decision. There are many times each day when we make choices affecting whether that door is open or closed.

In my experience the only way in which I can open that door regularly is through daily prayer. I have tried different times in the day to pray, but the only one that is effective for me is in the morning. Each and every day I ask Christ into my life, and ask for the grace to see his hand at work.

Today, may we look deeper into Jesus' words and hear the powerful message – that we have the choice to do good. He will be there to guide us with the power of his Spirit. However and whenever we may do it, today let us invite Jesus into our lives and open the door to Christ.

Vinaigrette of Life

If I took olive oil and red wine vinegar and put them together, what would I get? The basis for a salad dressing called vinaigrette. Is that all I need to do to make the vinaigrette? I know we could add some spices and herbs, but what else must I do with the oil and vinegar? Yes, I must shake them all up or blend them together. If however, after we mix it, we leave this vinaigrette to sit for a few hours, what happens? Yes, they separate out again into oil and vinegar. If you have ever been at dinner where vinaigrette is served, you know that you need to shake it all up again before pouring.

Oil on its own in a salad is not as good as vinaigrette, and vinegar on its own is not as good as vinaigrette. The blending of two ingredients together, the oil and the vinegar, makes a great dressing. I think this is great analogy for marriage.

Two separate substances are brought together and when they get shaken up and blended together they become something more than either of them could be on their own. They are better than they could ever be alone. However, if they do not take time to shake it all up, if they do not take time to blend into each other, then they will separate and become oil or vinegar again. Whether it be reading quietly in the same room or a romantic weekend vacation together, if they do not spend quality time together then they will separate out and drift apart.

This blending together or shaking it all up is what marriage is all about. This blending process is the process of loving, the process of loving one person and allowing yourself to be loved by one person.

I say process because it is never complete. Many of you are married for 5, 10, 25, 50 and some 60 years and you know that the wedding day was not all there was to marriage. Indeed the wedding day is only the beginning of this loving process. Each day you have the choice to blend or not. Each day you have the choice to love or not. Each day you have the choice to be loved or not. The process never ends.

One never reaches a point in the marriage and says, 'At last I have finally made it. I am completely married! After twenty five years I have finally arrived.' That is not the way it works.

Marriage is a process that takes us on a life's journey with no end. Each day we choose to love and be loved. The theme in today's first reading from Genesis and in the gospel is the covenant of marriage. Marriage is compared to two becoming one flesh.

Here we are reminded about the ideal of marriage and how we are called to be blended together to make a wonderful new existence. This image for the covenant of marriage is also meant to be an image of the covenant of God. Marriage is seen as a living witness of God's covenant with his people. While married people are called to be blended together within their own marriage, we are all called to be blended to Christ. We are all invited to allow the Spirit of Christ into our lives and so be blended into something new, something more than we could ever be on our own. In the same way that a married couple chooses to love each other we, as Christian disciples, can choose to love Christ and our neighbour. Like married life, this choice requires a commitment – a commitment to spend some quality time with one another. If we do not take this quality time with the Lord each day, then soon we will separate back to ourselves, like the oil from the vinegar.

Instead, we are called to choose Christ, allowing his Spirit to fill us and be blended into our every move and word. But we must be committed too. We need to commit time to the Lord each day.

We come here to this table each Sunday to be filled with the Lord and his goodness and that is wonderful. We agree to come as a community, to be all shaken up and blended together for another week. However, we know that this is not enough. We need to commit to some quality time with the Lord so that we can be blended with His Holy Spirit and become more than we could be on our own.

Whether we are married for 5 or 50 years, or whether we are divorced three times, or whether we are widowed, or whether we have never married, we are all called to be blended with Christ.

This week may we allow ourselves to be blended with Christ into the vinaigrette of life, where we allow ourselves to be loved by God through others and love God by loving others. This week along with Christ may we become the 'vinaigrette of life'.

Fire Fighters, Not Fire Spectators

A friend of mine is a firefighter with the City of Santa Clara and one day I went to visit him at the station house. I wanted to see how his job works. They have very nice quarters, with a living room, kitchen, dining room and sleeping area, too. Basically, the firehouse is like an ordinary house but bigger. Curious as to how my friend did his work, I asked, 'Tell me how this firefighting all happens.''When the alarm bell goes off we stop whatever we are doing and jump into our firefighting gear,' he said patiently. 'Beside the fire truck, each of the firefighter jumpsuit's lies waiting, with our boots already in place within the jumpsuit. We simply jump into the prepared gear and off we go. Sometimes we have to put on some gear in the truck because we were caught doing something in the garden or elsewhere. En route we are told what the state of the fire is, and we communicate with each other via our wireless headset system to decide how to approach the situation. 'So what happens then?' I asked. He responded, 'Depending on the size of the fire we either connect the hoses to the truck tank and/or to the nearest water hydrant. And then we deal with the fire.' 'How?' I asked. 'We go into the flames to find the direct source of the fire.' I stopped him mid-sentence, 'You go into the flames?' 'Yes. Duhhh! We go into the flames so we can get to the source of the fire.'

I thought to myself what a great analogy to being a Christian disciple. I mean, if we consider our entire life as a disciple to be an inferno, then our job is to enter into the flames to get to the direct source. (Now, for you literalists, of course I don't mean real flames of fire.) Sometimes I wonder if we stay on the outside, admiring the power or even beauty of the flames, but never entering the fire.

Can you imagine if the firefighters went to all the trouble of dressing up in their fire-proof gear, rushing to the fire and then stopping outside and watching the fire burn the building down? It doesn't make sense, does it? Well, I sometimes wonder if maybe we act more like fire-spectators than firefighters. I mean, we get all dressed up to come to Mass, we say all the right prayers, but when we get to the real fire of others' needs we stop and watch! We look and say, 'Oh look – someone is hungry! Oh look – someone is lonely! Oh look – someone is in need!' And then, we do not get involved!

Our parents need us to take care of them in their old age, but we shuffle them off to some strange place. Our children need our time to share their daily experiences, and we are too busy earning money or watching sports. Our neighbours, co-workers, or fellow-students need our assistance, yet we have too much to achieve for ourselves to help them.

Well, the reading from the Letter to the Hebrews is right on the button when it says that the sword of the truth pierces straight to the heart. In today's gospel Jesus makes no bones about his stand when the man asks him what he must do to get eternal life. Jesus says to sell everything and come and follow him. In other words, Jesus is saying only total commitment is acceptable. Wow! That is hard to hear. Total commitment!

It is not enough to just follow the commandments but we must be willing to lay down our lives for others. We must be willing to give up everything to follow the Lord. We must be willing to enter into the flames of life and be fully committed as disciples. Those flames are different for all of us. Some of us need to enter the flames of our parents' lives. Some of us need to enter the flames of our children's lives. Some of us need to enter the flames of the lives of our friends, co-workers or neighbours.

No matter whose flames we need to enter into, we are all called to enter into the flames of life so we can go straight to the source of the heat. We are all called not to be fire-spectators but fire fighters of this life we call Christian.

Branch of Weakness

Imagine yourself hiking through the woods on a trail that you know well. It is a dangerous trail but you know the danger spots. There are several narrow sections of the trail that you have fallen on before. You reach one of those sections and you fall again, because you were careless. As you sit in the mud of the trail you get mad at yourself because you should have known better. Just then, a gust of wind breaks a branch of a tree and the branch falls on you, pinning your legs to the ground. You try with all your strength but there is no way you can lift the heavy branch. You are not injured in any way – just stuck in the mud.[1]

Then you hear a voice of a man and only ten yards away you see this huge man, someone as big as the Incredible Hulk, walking by. All you have to do is call out and he will come and help. He is strong enough to lift the branch without much effort. But you do not call out; you feel stupid for getting yourself into this predicament. You should have known better! 'I have been down this path before and I should not have fallen again,' you think. You are mad at yourself and you are ashamed to ask for help. 'Besides, it does not hurt,' you argue. 'Maybe I can wiggle myself free from the heavy branch.'

The man remains within shouting distance but your pride will not allow you to call out. You remain trapped out of fear of appearing weak.

I think this story illustrates where we can often find ourselves on our path of life as a disciple. We know the trail very well, especially those narrow sections where we are vulnerable and weak. We have fallen at those places before. Even though we know the path, we fall because we get careless. Then we get mad at ourselves because we consider ourselves stupid for having fallen again. Then the branch of our vulnerabilities pins us down so we cannot rise above our failings.

But not far from us is the Lord Jesus, who is willing to lift our

---

Adapted from Jim Auer, *Celebration: An Ecumenical Worship Resource*, (Kansas City, Montana: National Catholic Reporter Company, Inc., October, 2003).

crosses and set us free from our weakness. But we must call out for forgiveness. We need to be willing to accept help. Yet, often we remain pinned by our weakness, trapped by our fear of appearing weak or stupid. Today's second reading of the Letter to the Hebrews assures us that we should not be fearful of the Lord. We ought to call out to him for mercy since he will be there to help and rescue us.

Jesus is not some distant, far-away God but a God who has walked this journey of human life and knows how difficult it is for all of us. He was tempted in every way we are, yet never sinned.

So let us confidently approach the throne of grace to receive mercy and favour and to find help in time of need. So, when we fall to that weakness we know so well, we get mad at ourselves for making that same mistake again. Whether it is gossiping about our friends, or cheating on an exam, or stealing those 'little' things from the office, or whether it is something even more significant, we are invited to call out to the Lord for help. He will be there and he will help us.Jesus will lift that branch of sin that has us pinned to the mud of our life. Christ will set us free. All we have to do is call out for help.

That all sounds fine, but how do we do that? First, we need to reflect on our lives and be honest about our human weakness. When we acknowledge our sins and ask God for help, he will forgive us. Then we are set free to live again. Then we can share the good news that Christ has saved us.

And through this sharing with others we can spread the good news that Christ is always ready to forgive us and all we have to do is ask for help.Yes, we come to this table each week and celebrate the reconciliation that Christ has won for us; but I wonder, do we share that good news with others?

This week, may we be open to acknowledging our weaknessand accepting God's forgiveness for ourselves. May we also be compassionate to others who are pinned down by their weakness and stuck in the mud of their lives. May our compassion bring healing to their lives, so that they can rise from their burdens as new people, whether they are weighed down by their weakness for lying, stealing, cheating or gossiping, or maybe, they are weak because of a failed marriage or doubting their faith. May we allow the Lord to set us free from our weaknessesand lift the branch of sin from our legs of faith.

Blind Spot

Recently I was driving down Lawrence Expressway and I wanted to change lanes, so I put on the turn indicator, looked in the mirror, and started to move into the next lane. At the last minute I turned and looked over my shoulder and just in time I saw a car in the lane into which I was trying to move. The car was driving in my blind spot! Fortunately, by looking over my shoulder I saw the car in time and avoided an accident.

Has that ever happened to you? Maybe you were not so lucky and you got into an accident. I certainly know lots of people who have had accidents like that. Isn't it true that no matter who is driving, we all have those blind spots? Sometimes I wonder if people don't drive in the spot intentionally to annoy others. In any case, we all have these blind spots when driving.

I also think this is true of life itself. I believe that we all have blind spots in our relationships. Sometimes we may think that others intentionally stand in them. Whether it is in our relationship with our spouse, or whether it is in our relationship with our children or parents, or whether it is in our relationship with our friends or co-workers, we all have those blind spots. The question is, what do we do about them?

In today's gospel we hear about Bartimaeus, who is blind. To fully understand this passage we need take this gospel , in context with last week's gospel because they are related. Jesus asks Bartimaeus the same question today as he asked last week of James and John: 'What do you want me to do for you?' Bartimaeus responds, 'Master, I want to see.' But remember last week, James and John responded, 'We want to sit one at your right hand and the other at your left in your kingdom.' They wanted glory!

Interestingly, James and John, who can see and are disciples, seek glory instead of wisdom or insight. The blind man, Bartimaeus, seeks sight. The irony here is that it is the disciples who are blind, or at the very least, they have a significant blind spot.

In some real sense, we are all like James and John; we have some blind spots in our lives that prevent us from growing. But instead of ignoring them like James and John, we are called to act like Bartimaeus, who acknowledges his blindness and calls out to Christ for healing and sight. We are invited to acknowledge our blind spots and call out to the Lord for healing.

Christ cannot heal those who do not want to be healed, or those who do not know they need to be healed. In the same way that we deal with blind spots in driving, we need to turn our head toward the blind spots in our lives, acknowledge their presence, and then deal with them. Pretending that we do not have blind spots does not make them disappear. Rather, it puts us on a more likely path of destructive behaviour. Christ invites us to admit our blind spots and come to him for healing.

This week, may we take just one of our blind spots and ask the Lord to heal it. Maybe that spot is in our relationship with our spouse, with whom we no longer see eye to eye on some issue. Maybe it is in our relationship with our parents or children, with whom we seem to argue about the slightest thing. Maybe it is in our relationship with co-workers or neighbours, with whom we cannot communicate effectively. Maybe that spot is within ourselves, some part of ourselves that we do not want to deal with, such as our anger, unhappiness, our need to be right or whatever. It is dangerous to ignore our blind spots, and unless we acknowledge them, we cannot ask Christ to help us heal them.

Today and this week, let us take just one of our many blind spots and acknowledge it before God, and ask him for healing.

Leading By Example

When I go to my brother's house I am always amazed to see how fast his children are growing. One thing that always strikes me – how much they are growing in likeness to my brother and his wife! I mean both in good ways and in some bad ways. In the beginning it was wonderful and novel. My niece would imitate their laughs and she was very funny. Then she would imitate their mannerisms. All her imitations are always with a slight exaggeration. The latest imitation that Daniella is doing is the 'shocked' look. All parents know how much children imitate what they see.

So, too, it is with our faith. They will imitate what they see. If we are not enthusiastic about our faith our children won't be either. Our children look to us for modeling our own faith. Sometimes, that is hard to believe and sometimes they seem to model other people, such as sports or pop stars. When addressing his young officers, General Dwight Eisenhower used to demonstrate the art of leadership with a simple piece of string. He would place a length of string in front of each officer and say, 'Pull the string and it will follow wherever you wish to lead it. Now push the string, and it goes nowhere at all.' Eisenhower slowly looked each officer in the eye and said, 'It's the same when it comes to leading people.'[1]

Well, I say to everyone present here today, it is the same when it comes to leading people in faith. We must lead by our faith-filled example. In the gospel passage today we hear Jesus respond to a trick question. In his normal, quick-witted way Jesus turns the table back on them. 'What is the first of all the commandments?' they ask. Jesus tells them that to love God is the most important and the second is to love your neighbour.

In others words, show others how Christ has transformed our lives. I really believe the greatest gift we can give children is the ability to say I am sorry. The reason I say this is because it says two things: 1) we can make mistakes and; 2) we can recover from mistakes.

If our children can see us, and hear us say 'I am sorry,' then I

---

1. Brian Cavanagh, *Fresh Packet of Sower's Seeds*, #28.

really believe they will get the message of Christianity: that no matter what we do God still loves us.

How much we love them will show them how much God loves them. We will become God's hands and feet in this world. We lead by our example and our children will come to know that Christ lives within us, and will come to recognise the Christ within every person around them.

Love one another and say 'I'm sorry.'

External Reality or Internal Reality

There is a common axiom that says, 'That's only the symbolic meaning!' A symbol seems not to enjoy the full status of truth or reality. Indeed our scientific and technological society demandsmeasurable and verifiable facts for proof of reality. And we have lots of religious symbols that cannot produce such evidence.[1] Yet our society is littered with symbols and we rely on them.

Who among us would not be horrified if a married man took off his wedding ring and smashed it in front of his wife with a hammer? Would we not understand that as a demonstration of a failing or failed marriage? Who among us, as American citizens would not be angered if I took the American flag and burned it in front of you? Indeed, of the students among us, who of us would not be angered if I took our school mascot and destroyed it before our eyes? Yes, our society is full of very powerful symbols and they mean a great deal to us.

And we as Catholics have many symbols on which we rely to express our faith. The Eucharist is the most powerful and poignant of those symbols. We say that the symbols of bread and wine are the body and blood of Christ. And we celebrate that here each Sunday.

In our gospel reading today, Jesus rails against symbols. He warns against those who 'parade in their robes and accept marks of respect in public and places of honour' and 'recite long prayers'.

Jesus is warning against the mere externals. In other words, our external actions ought to mirror our internal disposition. We ought to be the same on the inside as the outside. He complained against the scribes whose hearts were not in their prayer. And to emphasis his point he uses the example of a widow. This is significant because during Jesus' time, women were subservient to their husbands. They did not have a voice in society except through their man. So when a man died before his wife, the woman was considered voiceless and destitute. Indeed

---

1. Adapted from William F. Maestri, *Grace Upon Grace*, (Makati, Philippines: St Paul Publications, 1988) 212.

the very word, widow, *Almanah* (in Hebrew) has a root meaning of being the 'silent one'. So Jesus gives the 'silent one' the most powerful voice of all. He puts her at the centre to illustrate that the meaning of her life was determined by actions that came from her heart. Because she gave from her heart and not from her excess money, she is exemplified as a disciple.

We are all called to give from the heart and not just from our excess. So how do we do that this week? Maybe we are called to give more money and that is a good thing. But maybe we are also called to give something else. How about giving our very selves?

This week, why don't we try to do one new thing for others. I mean, for students, let's do something new for our parents, a chore around the house we have never done before, for example. Or at school, be a friend to someone with whom you are not currently friends. And adults, let's also do one new thing this week. It might be as simple as saying hello to someone at work with whom we never talk, or greeting neighbours whom we have never greeted before. Or maybe it is listening to a family member or friend who is really in need of a caring friend. Or perhaps, it is touching a person who desperately needs the human touch of love.

This week, let us find one *new* way to express our Christianity. And in so doing, bring the symbol of our faith alive in our actions. Then our words will be consistent with our actions and we will be like the widow whose actions speak louder than her voice could ever speak.

Now is the Time

Last week a friend of mine went to his doctor to get some medication for his sleep problems. The doctor wrote him a prescription for a new medication that he had never taken before. So he went home, took the medication and went to bed. He woke up in the emergency room at the local hospital; he had nearly died. He was allergic to the medication and had gone into pharmaceutical poisoning. Fortunately, another friend found him shortly after he had taken the medication, while he was convulsing and in shock. By the time the medical personnel arrived he had stopped breathing and his heart had stopped.Fortunately, with the speed and skill of the medical technicians, they were able to revive and stabilise my friend until he arrived at the hospital, where they injected him with the antidote to the medication.

He was discharged from the hospital several hours later with a clean bill of health. He had no brain damage, no permanent damage at all.While he does not have any memory of what happened, his body shows the marks of the trauma. He has a broken rib from them trying to restart his heart. His arms and legs are all bruised and his wrists are cut because they had to tie him down due to the convulsions. His mouth is badly cut because they had to stop him from swallowing his tongue. Other than those marks, he is no different physically.

However, he is now very different. He realises that his life has gone before him. He has been given a second chance. Now he is more thankful for the ordinary things of life, the simple gifts of health, family and friends. Now he does not take things so seriously. Now he forgives the past. Now he lives in the present. Now he eagerly looks forward to the future.

Do we need to come that close to death before we decide to live life in the present? Do we need to see our life pass in front of us before we acknowledge our need to let go of the past?

In today's scripture, we hear about the end times. The prophet Daniel envisions a time when good overcomes evil and the splendour of God shines brightly.

In the gospel we hear, in apocalyptic language, how the oppressive powers will be dethroned and how in the new world the faithful will rightfully be in charge. This language is intimidating and mysterious, but it is meant to encourage us, not to scare or frighten us. And remember, nobody will know the time or hour. Only the Father knows when our time is up.

Since we do not know when our time will come, may we live today as if it is our last. I am not saying that we be irresponsible and forget our real obligations. I am saying live as if there was no tomorrow. Listen carefully to God's call to be holy, and act now on his command to love one another.

Now is the time to forgive those age-old grudges. Now is the time to ask forgiveness from others we have hurt. Now is the time to repair broken relationships and talk to those family members or friends with whom we have lost touch, and let go of the reason we fell out of contact. Now is the time to reach out to others in need, maybe to that neighbour who has lost his spouse this year. Now is the time to talk to that student or co-worker-who always seems to be alone. Now is the time to be real about our Christian duty.

We do not need to wait until our life passes in front of us, as with my friend's close brush with death. We should not wait until tomorrow. Today is the moment. Now is the time!

The Truth Will Set Us Free

There is a story told of a king who had no children. When the king was getting old he invited all the children of his kingdom into his palace. Upon entering the Great Hall each child was given a small seed. 'The successor to my throne stands among you,' the king said, greeting children from all over his kingdom. 'Each of you has been given a seed. This seed will determine your future. You are to plant the seed, water it every day, and return here in one year with the fruits of your labour.'

Young Philip, one of the poorest children in the kingdom, rushed home and planted the seed in a pot full of soil. Every day he watered the soil faithfully and placed the pot where it could get the most sun. Days passed but nothing grew. Philip fertilised the soil but nothing seemed to help. Months passed, but the pot remained barren. Finally the day came when the king called all the children back to his palace with the harvest of their seeds. Philip had nothing to show and did not want to go. But his mother insisted saying, 'Philip, you did what you were asked to do. You have nothing to be ashamed of. Go to the palace and be honest with your results.' When Philip arrived at the palace, he was amazed by the dazzling flowers and plants all the other children had grown. Philip was embarrassed and cowered into the corner.

The king walked into the Great Hall, inspecting the flowers as he walked around. Philip held his breath as the king spotted him. 'You, in the corner there. Come here at once!' Philip reluctantly approached the king as the other children laughed at his pot full of dirt. 'What is your name?' the king asked. 'My name is Philip, your majesty,' answered Philip. The king stepped forward and bowed to Philip and named him the successor to his throne.

All the other children were confused. Then the king said, 'One year ago today I gave each of you a boiled seed that could not grow anything. Yet, today, I see every kind of plant that grows in the kingdom. Master Philip is the only one among you with the honesty and integrity to bring back an empty pot and face possible ridicule and reproach. Such integrity and respect for truth is a sign of a true King. I present to you King Philip.'[1]

---

1. Adapted from *Connections* (Mediaworks, Londonderry, NH: November, 2003)

Today we celebrate the Feast of Christ the King. Although this feast was given to us in 1925 by Pius XI to combat the growing belief in Nazism, communism and fascism, it is still worthwhile for us to focus on its message. The message is that Christ is King of the universe in all ways and his kingdom reigns forever. But in the words of Jesus from John's gospel: His kingdom is not of this world. His kingdom is based on truth and he came to testify to that truth. Christ lived that truth. Christ even died for that truth. Indeed Christ is the King of truth.

For our part, we are called to live in that kingdom here and now. We are called to live in truth in all ways. I realise that this not always easy, and often we will be ridiculed for attempting to do so. Sometimes we will be even persecuted for doing do. But if we are to call ourselves Christians then we must become bearers of the truth and be willing to be held accountable to the truth.

The truth will challenge us, the truth will disappoint and hurt us, the truth will call us to integrity and honesty, and the truth will set us free. To live the truth we need to practise it in our own lives first. May we be humble enough to know and acknowledge our weakness. May we have the honesty and integrity to bring back an empty pot when our labours produce no flowers. May we be prepared to always tell the full truth, whether it be in the office, in our school or at home, whether it be with family, friends or co-workers, whether it be about ourselves or about others.

May we become known as bearers of the truth and thus set each other free.